SHERINGHAM AT WAR
100 YEARS ON

EDITED BY PETER FARLEY & TIM GROVES

DESIGNED & PRODUCED BY:

OUT OF THE BOX PUBLISHING

Sheringham World War One Centenary
Commemoration and Remembrance Project

CONTENTS

First published in Great Britain in 2018 by Out of the Box Publishing Limited, 1 Stone Beck Lane, Briston, Melton Constable, Norfolk NR24 2PS on behalf of Sheringham World War One Centenary Commemoration and Remembrance Project. Email: info@outoftheboxpublishing.co.uk. Web site: www.outoftheboxpublishing.co.uk.

Designed and produced by Martyn Barr. Printed and bound in Great Britain by Wyndeham Grange Limited, Southwick.

British Library Cataloguing in Publication Data
A catalogue record for this book is available from the British Library.

ISBN 978-0-9956667-3-3

The poppy installation in the moat in the Tower of London in 2014 –
Bloodswept Lands and Seas of Red – set the tone for our national commemoration

FOREWORD

As Martyn Barr so ably describes in his excellent book '*The Lost Generation*', very sadly the First World War did not turn out to be the 'war to end war'. However, it is absolutely right that one hundred years on, we are commemorating the tragic loss of life and the selfless sacrifice of so many in that most appalling of conflicts. Sheringham was not spared its share of the sacrifice borne by the nation a hundred years ago. Hardly a family in the town would have been unaffected by the First World War, as indeed were almost all the villages, towns and cities in Great Britain, as well as in British dominions and colonies overseas. Not only did so many inhabitants of the town lose their lives in the conflict but Sheringham entered the history books on 19th January 1915 by becoming the first civilian target to be hit in a Zeppelin – L4 airship raid when, at 8.30pm that evening, a house in Wyndham Street was bombed.

Personally, I am delighted to have been invited to write the foreword to this commemorative publication, not only because I have so many happy memories of summers in Sheringham, but also because Wyndham Street is just around the corner from the first house that I ever owned. It is such a privilege to share in Sheringham's history and make a small contribution to the town's First World War commemorations.

I believe the poppy installation in the moat in the Tower of London in 2014 – *Bloodswept Lands and Seas of Red* – set the tone for our national commemoration, and communities up and down the country have shaped their commemorations in their own way – Sheringham is no exception to this. The programme of events in which the lives of townsfolk are remembered and commemorated, is most imaginative and comprehensive, stretching from Beeston Regis, to Upper Sheringham and, of course, in Sheringham itself.

We have all grown up with seeing names on the town War Memorial but this year those names are being given a personality again, as so many stories of past sacrifice and service are researched and told once more. The First World War may not have ended wars – sadly it was followed by a second global conflict and a score of other conflicts since. The conflict of 1914–1918 marked a watershed in so many ways, not least the changing role of women in our society. Today, brave men and women still put on the uniforms of our armed forces and emergency services, in order to protect our freedom and wellbeing both at home and abroad.

In this book, we salute the memory of those who have served and fallen on behalf of our nation. In remembering them, we give thanks for all that they did for us a hundred years ago. We also give thanks for those who continue to serve our country today. Moreover, we can all join together, while remembering the past, to hope, pray and work now, for a better future for the generations to come. I congratulate Sheringham for this magnificent commemoration and wish every success to the events planned around Armistice 2018.

Richard Dannatt
General The Lord Dannatt GCB CBE MC DL
Chief of the General Staff 2006–2009
Constable of HM Tower of London 2009–2016

PARTNERS

The following organisations are partners in the Sheringham World War One Centenary Commemoration and Remembrance Project:

Beeston Regis Parish Council
Lighthouse Community Church
North Norfolk Railway
RNLI Sheringham
Sheringham and Cromer Choral Society
Sheringham Carnival
Sheringham Churches Together
Sheringham Dementia Friendly Group
Sheringham Golf Club
Sheringham in Bloom
Sheringham Little Theatre
Sheringham Museum at The Mo
Sheringham Primary School
Sheringham Society
Sheringham Town Council
Sheringham Woodfields School
St Peter's Parish Church

Life Church
Morley Club
Our Lady and St Joseph's Church
Salvation Army Sheringham Corps
Sheringham Branch Royal British Legion
Sheringham Chamber of Trade
Sheringham Coastwatch
Sheringham Fire Brigade
Sheringham High School
Sheringham Library
Sheringham Medical Practice
Sheringham Police
Sheringham Shantymen
Sheringham Tesco
Sheringham Women's Institute
St Andrew's Methodist Church
Upper Sheringham Parish Council

SPONSORS

We are grateful to our sponsors, who have financially supported the publication of *Sheringham at War – 100 years on*. We respectfully request that readers take time to view their advertisements.

Carousel Amusements
Hayes & Storr
Morley Club
North Norfolk Railway
Sheringham Chamber of Trade
Sheringham Town Council
Silver & Ward
The Ashcroft Family
The Family of Marlborough Picton Pegg

Clapham & Collinge
Lawrence's Garages
Norfolk Homes
Red Lobster Gallery
Sheringham Golf Club
Sheringham Trawler
The Family of A Bullen
The Family of Harry Collings

FROM THE AUTHORS

It was a great privilege to compile *Sheringham at War – 100 years on*. We hope it is a fitting tribute to all those in Sheringham, Beeston Regis and Upper Sheringham who were caught up in the conflict which was World War One.

We are extremely grateful to all those who, in any way, supplied material for this publication. Many thanks to Sheringham Museum, where volunteers have scoured their extensive archives to make available a wealth of material, including many rare and unique images,

We are especially indebted to Jane Crossen, Iain Turner and Martyn Barr for their painstaking work in researching and providing much of the copy for this publication. We are also grateful to Out of the Box Publishing Limited (**www.ootbshop.co.uk**) for doing a really first class job in producing and publishing this book.

Our thanks also to people like Lord Dannatt for his inspiring foreword and Bruno Peek LVO OBE OPR, Pageant Master, for giving us permission to use material from his *'Battle's Over'* publicity.

The team responsible for the website **www.roll-of-honour.com** have done a wonderful job researching many war memorials throughout the country, providing basic details on those named on the Beeston Regis, Sheringham and Upper Sheringham memorials. This was a very valuable source of information, which often kick-started our research. We have taken great care throughout this publication to ensure accuracy and to acknowledge copyright holders of images wherever possible. However, we apologise for any errors or omissions and will be pleased to correct these at the next available opportunity.

Peter Farley and Tim Groves

© *Sheringham Museum Trust. By kind permission of Sheringham Museum.*

A WAR TO END WAR?

In the early years of the 20th century, a war between the nations of Europe seemed inevitable. When it eventually came in 1914, it was greeted with considerable enthusiasm. Many military and political leaders thought that a short, sharp war would bring stability to world affairs. But it lasted four long years and its outcome was in doubt even to the very end.

It was a truly global war. Fighting didn't just take place on the muddy fields of Belgium and France, but in the deserts of the Middle East and the jungles of Africa, on the oceans and in the mountains.

The Great War, as it was known then, cost the lives of around 17 million military personnel and civilians. By its conclusion in 1918, empires had toppled, three crowned heads of Europe had been deposed and new countries had come into being.

ORIGINS

Britain's navy was the envy of the world. In 1906, it launched a new battleship – *HMS Dreadnought* – bigger, faster and with more firepower than any other warship. Soon Germany was building its own super ships and a fierce race for supremacy of the world's oceans began.

Other European governments were also expanding their armed forces and jockeying for position on the world's stage. Relations between Europe's leaders became increasingly strained and war seemed inevitable. The situation was made more complicated by the tangled web of pacts and promises that bound European countries to each other in the event of war. In the end, it was the assassination of a little-known Austro-Hungarian Royal in a far-flung corner of Europe that plunged the world into global conflict.

A SPARK TO A FLAME

No-one knows for sure whether the Serbian government was involved in the assassination of the heir to the Austro-Hungarian throne, Archduke Franz Ferdinand. But Austria-Hungary wanted to teach Serbia a lesson and gain a stronger foothold in the Balkans, bolstered by a cast iron guarantee from Kaiser Wilhelm that Germany would support them.

On 28 July 1914, Austria-Hungary declared war on Serbia. Russia, which had a treaty with Serbia, started to mobilise its vast army. Germany viewed the Russian mobilisation as an act of war against its ally Austria-Hungary and declared war on Russia. Two days later it declared war on France.

Britain's agreement with France did not compel it to support its ally in war, but it was sympathetic to France's plight. It was Germany's invasion of Belgium that finally tipped the balance. Britain had a longstanding treaty to protect Belgian neutrality and so sent Germany an ultimatum to withdraw its troops immediately.

As the British Foreign Secretary, Sir Edward Grey, waited for the midnight deadline, he declared: *"The lamps are going out all over Europe. We shall not see them lit again in our time."* There was no response and, on 4 August 1914, Britain declared war on Germany.

A CALL TO ARMS

Perhaps surprisingly, the British people did not react with dismay at the thought of war. Most lived quiet, uneventful lives. War was seen as a big adventure – a chance for young men to be heroes, win glory and see the world. And, in any event, most people thought it would all be over by Christmas.

Field Marshal Lord Kitchener, the Secretary of State for War, feared a long drawn-out conflict with many casualties. Germany had five million men ready to fight. Britain's regular army was tiny in comparison – just 200,000 men. A vast army of volunteers would be needed.

Propaganda posters were put up across Britain. The response vastly exceeded Kitchener's expectations. Within two months, 750,000 men had volunteered. Despite a minimum recruitment age of 18, boys as young as 13 lied about their age or gave false names so that they could join up. Military service promised opportunity, excitement and travel and, for many, offered a break from the grinding poverty of everyday life. Recruits could expect regular pay, proper food and clothing, and accommodation in barracks that for some was better than the often squalid living conditions back home.

It was soon realised that men would be more willing to join up if they could serve with people they knew. 'Pals' battalions were made up of workmates, friends or men from specific occupations. Civic pride and community spirit prompted cities to compete with each other to attract new recruits.

Pals battalions certainly increased the number of volunteers, but in the bloody battles that followed, the price paid was immense, both by the men themselves and the decimated communities they left behind.

WOMEN STEP UP TO THE MARK

The massive exodus of men to join Kitchener's army left Britain short of skilled labour. Their places were largely taken by women. As the war

Ruins of St Martin's Church and Cloth Hall in Ypres, Belgium

dragged on, women took on a wide variety of jobs, from train driving to coal mining. Many worked as nurses near the front lines. The Women's Auxiliary Army Corps was set up in 1917 and sent many women across to the battlefields of France. There they helped with administration, training and cooking, freeing up more men to fight at the Front. Liberal politician David Lloyd George, who would later become Prime Minister, enlisted the help of thousands of women to work in munitions factories, where they worked for long hours handling dangerous chemicals and explosives.

In 1917, with food convoys being specifically targeted by German U-boats, Britain started to run low on food. A Ministry of Food was set up and women were encouraged to join the Women's Land Army to help farmers.

THE END GAME

Throughout August and September 1918, Allied troops continued to advance steadily across France, gaining more and more ground. The enemy defences crumbled. By early October, the Germans were in retreat, freeing much of occupied France and Belgium.

The following month, Germany was in turmoil. There was a mutiny in the navy and riots on the streets. Many people were weakened or dying from the Spanish Flu epidemic. The Kaiser was forced to abdicate and flee the country. Germany's allies in the Central Powers had already made peace.

During the early morning of 11 November 1918, in a train carriage in the Forest of Compiègne near the front line, German and Allied leaders signed an armistice – an agreement to stop fighting. Later that day, on the eleventh hour of the eleventh day of the eleventh month, the guns fell silent. The First World War was over.

IN LOVING MEMORY

Over 900,000 soldiers from Britain and its colonies died in the First World War. Many more were badly injured. Few returning soldiers, sailors and airmen would ever forget the horrors they witnessed.

Soldiers were generally buried near to where they fell by their comrades. Many were never found, literally blown to pieces by the artillery fire, and recorded as 'missing in action'.

After the war, huge cemeteries were built alongside the battlefields. Row after row of headstones recorded the name of the dead soldier, their rank and regiment and a simple message; each headstone the same – in death, none more important than the other.

In the years following the Great War, villages, towns and cities across Britain set up their own memorials, inscribed with the names of those who had died. And every year since, people across the country have observed two minutes' silence to honour the war dead.

A 'LOST GENERATION'?

The First World War lasted four long years and heralded a modern age of warfare, with new fighting methods and technologies that impacted an entire generation of young men and women.

As a result of the killing fields of Belgium and France, hundreds of local communities across the length and breadth of the country lost all their men in a single stroke. After the war, many felt that 'the flower of youth' and 'the best of the nation' had been destroyed.

Even those that survived were, in many respects, 'lost'. Jobs were scarce, soldiers roamed the streets begging, many suffered mentally and some were simply hidden away in back rooms and institutions for fear of upsetting a population eager to distance itself from the horrors and scarcities of war. Governments, too, started ignoring their war heroes, who rapidly became embittered and disillusioned with those in authority.

For the 'lost generation', the world had changed forever.

Extracted from 'The Lost Generation' by Martyn Barr and reproduced with kind permission.

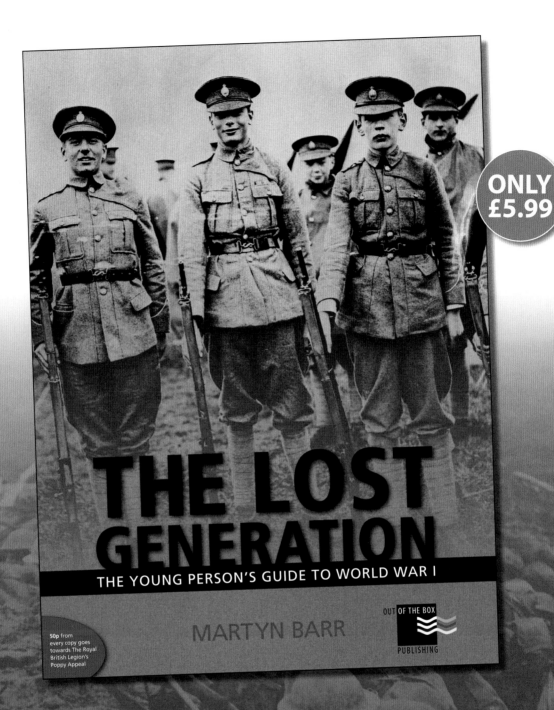

ONLY £5.99

THE LOST GENERATION

THE YOUNG PERSON'S GUIDE TO WORLD WAR I

50p from every copy goes towards The Royal British Legion's Poppy Appeal

MARTYN BARR

OUT OF THE BOX PUBLISHING

Written especially for today's generation of young people (and a great read for adults too), this richly illustrated guide charts the story of the First World War, from its origins in a far-flung corner of Europe to its bloody and bitter conclusion.

MEET THE AUTHOR

Award-winning author Martyn Barr will be signing copies of the book on 10th/11th November in Sheringham. Please see **www.ootbshop.co.uk** for venues and times.

Sponsored by:

Available from local stores and the Sheringham Museum or online at **www.ootbshop.co.uk**.

THE FALLEN

Seventy-five residents of Beeston Regis and Sheringham are listed on the Sheringham War Memorial, as having given their lives in World War One. A further two are also listed on the Beeston Regis memorial in All Saints Church and another eight are listed on the memorial at Upper Sheringham. However, we want to honour all those who served with the armed forces in the conflict. This number includes conscientious objectors, some of whom (as you will discover) were decorated for valour.

Lord Dannatt made this comment in his foreword:

"We have all grown up with seeing names on the town War Memorial but this year those names are being given a personality again, as so many stories of past sacrifice and service are researched and told once more."

It has been our privilege to find out all we can about them, and we hope that our work will give readers an insight into all we owe our forebears. More detailed stories of some of these men are given later.

Researched and compiled by Iain Turner and Peter Farley

SHERINGHAM WAR MEMORIAL

1914

JOHN R KEMPSON

Midshipman, *HMS Hawke*, Royal Navy. Lost with his ship on 15th October 1914, aged 17. The first Sheringham casualty. He has no known grave but is commemorated on Chatham Naval Memorial, Kent.

SIDNEY L SAUL

Private S4/035425, "A" Supply Company, Army Service Corps. Died of convulsions at the Thorpe St Andrew Asylum on 26th December 1914, aged 36. He is buried in The Rosary Cemetery, Norwich.

DOUGLAS WARDLEWORTH

Lieutenant, Royal Army Medical Corps, who was drowned swimming at Le Havre on 24th October 1914, aged 34. He was a general practitioner in Sheringham. His son Edmund was born the same day he died. He was buried in Ste Marie Cemetery, Le Havre.

1915

FREDERICK J APPLEGATE

Private 3027 in 1/5th (Territorial Force), Norfolk Regiment. Died at sea on 9th November 1915, aged 24, on board *HMHS Devhana*, a hospital ship en route to the UK. Frederick is commemorated on the Helles Memorial, Turkey.

VICTOR C CRASKE

Private 1447, 1/5th Battalion (Territorial Force), Norfolk Regiment. Killed in action at Gallipoli on 21st August 1915, aged 19. Member of the Sheringham Salvation Army Band. He has no known grave and is commemorated on the Helles Memorial, Turkey.

GEORGE E BANE

Lance Corporal, 7494 George Bane was born in Southrepps in 1890 and the 1891 census showed his mother, Ellen, as the head of the household and a charwoman. She was aged 29 and had three children, Flowerday (6), James (3) and George (8 months). Living with them were Ellen's mother, Charlotte, and her brother, George, who was a farm labourer.

Sadly, Ellen died in 1893, the cause not being known, and the next sight we have of the family is in 1901 when we see that James (now 15) and George (12) were inmates at the West Beckham Poorhouse. We can only guess at the misery they had been through and it is no surprise to see that, by the 1911 census, George was a private serving with the 2nd Battalion, The Norfolk Regiment in 'India and Ceylon'. He was not alone in seeking security, regular pay and a good diet in the military.

He served in Mesopotamia and, following a number of costly actions, the remainder of his battalion marched to Kut-al-Amara with orders to hold the town until reinforcements arrived and spent Christmas 1915 under the most appalling conditions. Rations were soon depleted and they were reduced to a daily ration of horse or mule meat. Reinforcements did not arrive and on the 29th April 1916, after 146 days of the siege, Kut surrendered and those left alive were made prisoners of war. Their treatment was not good and many more died of maltreatment and disease.

George wrote to his brother James from his PoW camp saying *"I do not feel very well at present. You might send me some chocolate and toffee by return post or as quick as you can."*

On 5th September 1916 George finally succumbed to 'Dysentery and Malaria' and died at Yarbaschi Camp, as a prisoner of war (aged 26). The translation of the Turkish report of his death says that he *"died peacefully in the presence of his doctor and nurses. Buried by his comrades."* His grave is in the Baghdad (North Gate) War Cemetery.

GEORGE DENNIS

Able Seaman 165784 (CH), Royal Navy. He died on 10th June 1915, aged 40 on board a motor torpedo boat, *HMTB 12*, when it was sunk by a German submarine in the North Sea off Harwich. He left a widow and three children and is buried in All Saints Churchyard, Upper Sheringham.

SIDNEY DYBALL

Private 20656, 1st Battalion, Essex Regiment. He died on 13th August 1915 (aged 25) on board *HMT Royal Edward*, a troopship. *Royal Edward* was carrying 1,350 troops and a crew of 220, to the Dardenelles. Just off the island of Kandeloussa, the ship was hit by a torpedo launched from *UB 14*. The boat sank within six minutes and 864 men were lost, including Sidney Dyball. He has no known grave and is commemorated on the Helles Memorial, Turkey.

JAMES FUNNELL

Private 15529, 9th Battalion, Norfolk Regiment. Born in 1890, he was the son of Robert and Margaret Funnel, who lived at Chapel of Ease Cottage, Sheringham. He was an apprentice motor mechanic, who enlisted in 9th Battalion of the Norfolk Regiment at Norwich and ended up in the Ypres Salient. He died of gunshot wounds (aged 20) on 24th October 1915. He is buried in Lijssenthoek Military Cemetery, Poperinge, West-Vlaanderen, Belgium.

HERBERT J KNIGHTS

Born in Horsford on 24th July 1898, he was the son of Thomas Knights of 3 Weston Terrace, Sheringham. He enlisted in the Royal Navy as a boy third class and was sent for training at *HMS Ganges*, the Royal Navy Training Establishment at Shotley, Suffolk. During his training, he was taken ill and died on 4th June 1915, aged 16 years. He is buried in the Shotley Royal Naval Cemetery in Suffolk.

FREDERICK A MORTIMER

Born in Sheringham in 1883, he was the son of Francis Mortimer of 'Ennerdale', Cromer Road, Sheringham. He enlisted as a private in 7th Battalion of the Norfolk Regiment, at Norwich and went to France in May 1915. On 13th October 1915 (aged 32 years) he was reported missing in action, during the Battle of Loos. He was one of 226 men from 7th Battalion who were killed or reported missing in action that day. He is commemorated on the Loos Memorial, Pays de Calais, France.

CHARLES H SHEPHERD

Born in West Beckham in 1892, he was the son of William and Susan Shepherd. A farm labourer, living at Sheringham Road, West Beckham, he enlisted in the Norfolk Regiment and was posted to the 2nd Battalion in December 1912. In November 1914, his battalion embarked for Mesopotamia. He died on 6th February 1915 (aged 21 years) of an appendicitis at a military hospital in Basra. He was buried in the Basra War Cemetery. Basra, Iraq.

FREDERICK E TURNEY

Born in Bourne End, Buckinghamshire, he later moved to Sheringham. He was the son of Mary Adderson of Priory Villas, Beeston. He enlisted in the 5th Battalion of the Oxfordshire & Buckinghamshire Light Infantry. He was killed on 25th September 1915 (aged 19 years) at the second Battle of Bellewaarde Ridge. This was a disastrous diversionary attack launched to distract German attention from the Battle of Loos. He has no known grave and is commemorated on the Ypres (Menin Gate) Memorial Belgium.

JAMES J TURNEY

Elder brother of Fredrick Turney above, he was born in Dalston, Middlesex. He was the son of Mary Adderson of Priory Villas, Beeston. He enlisted in the 7th Battalion of the Regiment in London. He was killed in action on 13th October 1915 (aged 23 years), when the 7th Battalion were part of the 35th Brigade that tried to take the Hulluch Quarries, which were held by the Germans, who repelled the attack. He has no known grave and is commemorated on the Loos Memorial, Pas de Calais, France.

Another of those who fell that day, whose body was never recovered and is also commemorated on the Loos Memorial, was the war poet Charles Sorley. In '*When You See Millions of the Mouthless Dead*', he wrote:

"…Say only this, "They are dead." Then add thereto,
"Yet many a better one has died before."
Then, scanning all the o'ercrowded mass, should you
Perceive one face that you loved heretofore,
It is a spook. None wears the face you knew.
Great death has made all his for evermore."

THOMAS WATTS

Born in Edinburgh, he was the son of James and Emma Watts and lived in Barchams Yard, Sheringham. He worked as a golf caddy and enlisted at Norwich in the 2nd/4th Battalion of the Norfolk Regiment. He died in England on 12th November 1915, aged 22, and is buried in Cambridge City Cemetery. No details of his death could be found.

WILLIAM J WILKINSON

Little is known of William J Wilkinson. Some sources say he was a dental surgeon from New South Wales, and even that Queen Mary was one of his patients. He enlisted as a second lieutenant in the 3rd Battalion attached to 2nd Battalion of the Leicestershire Regiment. He was killed in action on 25th September 1915, the first day of the Battle of Loos. At 5.48 am that day, a British mine was detonated under the German lines, and the battle itself started at 6.00 am. As well as the enemy's guns, the troops had to contend with gas. William has no known grave, and is commemorated on the Loos Memorial, Pas de Calais, France.

1916

WILLIAM BROUGHTON

Born 1887 in Cromer, he was the son of James William and Louisa Broughton, who at the time of his death lived at Weston Street, Sheringham. After first being employed as a telegraph messenger, in February 1905 he was appointed as a sub office postmaster at Sheringham Corner. In May 1913, he transferred as a postman to London and lived in Bayswater. He joined the 1st/8th Battalion, London Regiment (Post Office Rifles), going to France on 18th March 1915. He was killed in

Dedication of the Sheringham War Memorial

THEREAS BULLEN

Thearus George Leonard Bullen was born on 27th December 1892 (notice the first variation of his name). Aged 8 and living with his parents at Cabbage Court, Reepham, his name is given as Thureasy L Bullen. At the National Archive, his medal index card listing refers to him as Theereas G Bullen. These variations in his Christian name prompted one commentator to observe that *"the family seems to have been fairly fluid with the spelling"*.

Thereas (as the memorial refers to him as) was a private in the 9th Battalion of the Norfolk Regiment, serving in France, when on 16th October 1916, aged 23, he was killed in action during the Battle of the Somme. He is commemorated on the Thiepval Memorial, having no known grave. The memorial commemorates more than 72,000 men of the British and South African forces who died during the Somme offensive of 1916, who have no known grave.

On 16th October 1916, the 9th Battalion of the Norfolks captured the north western part of Mild Trench and held it against a German attack at nightfall. Their exploits are detailed in a private letter from a Lieutenant Cubitt: *"For 48 hours, with water up to our knees, soaked to the skin, practically no water to drink, and dead beat, those splendid boys 'stood to', fought, and bombed, and held on. It was glorious to see how when one man was killed another took his place, and, when he fell, a third man. They were all heroes."*

The War Diary notes there were 248 killed that day (nine officers and 239 other ranks).

ALAN R DYBALL

Alan Dyball was born in Norwich in 1894 and was joined in 1896 by his younger brother, Harold. His father, Frederick, was a draper and his mother, Mary Ann, looked after Frederick (the eldest son) and his two younger brothers. The 1901 census shows the family were living in Sheringham and they had a servant, Elizabeth Cutting. Alan attended the local school and then was educated at Paston Grammar School (now Paston Sixth Form College) in North Walsham.

By April 1911, the family had moved to Montague Crescent at the top end of South Street. Alan's older brother, Frederick, was a schoolmaster and Alan was employed as a clerk (rate collector). They had a different servant now – Alice Baldwin – who was 16.

Alan enlisted in Cambridge and was posted to the 8th Battalion, the Suffolk Regiment where he was promoted to lance corporal. The battalion was involved in the actions to capture the Thiepval Ridge during the Battle of the Somme. This was the first major offensive conducted by Gough's Reserve Army and the attackers faced a well-fortified enemy position and determined resistance. The final British objectives were not reached until the Battle of the Ancre Heights (1st October – 11th November).

During these actions Alan was injured and died of his wounds (aged 22 years) on 29th September 1916. He is buried in the Abbeville Community Cemetery Extension, Somme, France.

---

action on 20th May 1916, aged 29 years, at the Battle of Festubert. He is commemorated on the Arras Memorial, Arras, France. Interestingly, probate was granted to his father, with his effects listed as £197 10s. 0d, worth nearly £17,000 today.

WALTER W COOPER

Born in Sheringham, the son of Levi and Susannah Cooper of Richmond House, Priory Road, Sheringham. He enlisted in the 8th Battalion of the Norfolk Regiment. He was killed on 19th May 1916 (aged 21 years), during the Battle of Fromelles. He was one of over 1,400 British soldiers killed there and has no known grave. Interestingly, it seems that Adolf Hitler, then a corporal in the 16th Bavarian Reserve Infantry Regiment, also took part in the battle. Walter is commemorated on the Thiepval Memorial, Somme, France.

JOHN F FORD

Probably Frederick John Ford, private 24753, 7th Battalion, Suffolk Regiment. He was a farm labourer. Killed in action on 12th October 1916, aged 21, in the attack on Bayonet Trench. He has no known grave and is commemorated on Thiepval Memorial, Somme France.

WILLIAM M GIDNEY

Born in Sheringham in 1878 to James and Martha Gidney of Lansdowne, Waterbank Road, Sheringham. He was a bricklayer's labourer and enlisted in the 2nd Battalion, Bedfordshire Regiment. He was killed in action on 12th October 1916, aged 36 years, possibly at the Battle of Le Transloy, the final offensive of the British Expeditionary Force on the Somme. He has no known grave and is commemorated on the Thiepval Memorial, Somme, France.

EDWARD H LINDER

Little is known of Edward Linder except he was born in Rushall, Norfolk and was a fruit salesman. He enlisted in 2nd Battalion of Royal Warwickshire Regiment and was killed in action near Albert on 23rd April 1916, aged 30. He is buried in Citadel New Military Citadel Cemetery. Fricourt, on the Somme.

WALTER T MORRIS

Born in Sheringham, his parents were Thomas and Lavinia Morris of Ivy Cottage, West Cliff, Sheringham. His father, who died in 1918, was the chief coastguard at Sheringham. Walter enlisted in Norwich with the 7th Battalion of Norfolk Regiment. He died of his wounds, aged 25, at home on 3rd November 1916 and is buried in All Saints Churchyard, Upper Sheringham.

ROBERT W SADLER

Born in Sheringham, the son of Mrs W Sadler, of Wyndham Street, Sheringham. He enlisted in Norwich with the 8th Battalion of the Norfolk Regiment. He was killed in action on 19th July 1916, aged 24 years, in the attack on Delville Wood. A German officer who fought there, stated that *"Delville Wood had disintegrated into a shattered wasteland of shattered trees, charred and burning stumps, craters thick with mud and blood, and corpses,*

ROBERT C MIDDLETON

Robert died a month before his 23rd birthday, whilst serving as a stoker aboard *HMS Hampshire*, when the cruiser hit a mine in Scapa Flow in the Orkneys, on 5th June 1916. He was one of a crew of 655, only 12 of whom survived when the vessel sank. He had lived with his parents, Henry and Elizabeth Middleton, in Upton Villa, Augusta Street, Sheringham.

Much has been written, fact and conjecture, about the sinking of *HMS Hampshire*, because among those who also perished was Britain's War Secretary, Lord Kitchener of Khartoum. The sinking happened when the vessel struck a mine while tackling a force nine gale, less than two miles off shore. Kitchener, one of the key figures in World War One, together with a delegation of 81 military officers, politicians and their staff (all of whom were killed), was travelling from Scapa Flow for talks with the Tsar of Russia in Archangel.

Kitchener's image was immortalised on the recruiting poster which inspired many young patriotic Britons to go on an adventure to 'beat the Hun' and be home in time for Christmas!

We are grateful to Nena Woods, Robert's great niece, for supplying information and pictures of Robert and his memorial plaque (left).

ALBERT BAYFIELD

Albert Bayfield was born in the village of Hunworth, near Holt, in about 1876, the son of Ellis and Bridgett Bayfield. By trade he was a bricklayer and, in around 1897, he married Eliza. By the census of 1911 they lived on Beeston Road in Sheringham with their six children.

His wife, Eliza, was not at all happy when he decided to enlist and leave her and their (by then) seven children to fend for themselves. Albert would not have had to serve, but chose to following a trip to the pub. He was a member of a local shooting team and regarded as being a fine shot. He was remembered by the family as a kindly man. His skill as a bricklayer was such that he was employed in the building of St Peter's Church. He did, however, have a fiery temper.

Initially, he was posted to the Middlesex Regiment and would almost certainly not have been sent to the Front. He would have more likely been posted to one of the ports or guarding the hospitals or rear depots. Unfortunately there seems to have been an incident on the parade ground prior to embarkation where a young officer had made a remark about his uniform and Albert threw down his rifle. After a short time in a nearby military prison, he was transferred to the 13th Battalion, The Royal Fusiliers (City of London Regiment) who were bound for the Front – five kilometres south east of Arras.

Albert was killed in action on 10th/11th April 1917 (aged 40) during the First Battle of the Scarpe at Monchy-le-Preux. By its conclusion on 16th May, the Battle of Arras had claimed 160,000 British casualties. Albert has no known grave and is commemorated on the Arras Memorial, Pas de Calais.

As an afternote, Eliza must have eventually forgiven him, for her gravestone in the Sheringham Town Cemetery says:

"In sacred memory of Eliza Bayfield who died March 1st 1950 aged 73. Also her loving husband Albert, killed in action April 9th 1917 aged 40. Reunited."

corpses everywhere. In places they were piled four deep." Robert has no known grave and is commemorated on the Thiepval Memorial, Somme, France. He was grieved by his parents and four sisters.

CYRIL P WATSON

Born in Burnley, he was the son of Brigadier General A G Watson of the East Lancashire Regiment, who served in Bengal, fought in the Zulu War 1879 and the Afghan War 1880 and who subsequently retired to Sheringham. Cyril joined his father's old regiment and served as a captain. He was killed in action on 1st July 1916, the first day of the Battle of the Somme (aged 32). This proved to be the bloodiest day in the history of the British Army and one of the most infamous days of World War One. The British forces suffered 57,470 casualties, including 19,240 fatalities and gained just three square miles of territory. He has no known grave and is commemorated on the Thiepval Memorial, Somme, France.

CHARLIE WELLS

Company sergeant major of the 8th Battalion of the East Surrey Regiment, born in Coltishall, Norfolk, in 1888 to Nellie and Charles Wells. In

1913, aged 21, he married Elsie Laura Todd at Beeston Regis. Like Captain Watson, he was killed in action on 1st July 1916, the first day of the Battle of the Somme, aged 27. He has no known grave and is commemorated on the Thiepval Memorial, Somme, France.

1917

MATTHEW J BROWN

Born on 27th September 1895, his parents were Benjamin (fish merchant) and Matilda Brown, living at Stream Cottage, Beeston Road, Sheringham, one of a family of thirteen. Working as a labourer, he enlisted in the 7th Battalion of the Norfolk Regiment in Norwich. He was killed in action on 28th April 1917 (aged 21 years) during the Battle of Arras at Monchy Woods. He has no known grave and is commemorated on the Arras Memorial, Pas de Calais.

WALTER CHASTNEY

Born in Sheringham around 1896, his parents were Charles (bricklayer) and Jemima Chastney. He lived in 'Cottage 2, near the Railway Bridge', Sheringham. He enlisted in 7th Battalion Norfolk Regiment. He was killed in action on 28th April 1917, aged 21 years, during the Battle of Arras at Monchy Woods. He has no known grave and is commemorated on the Arras Memorial, Pas de Calais.

RICHARD C COX

Born in 1881 in Sheringham, a fish hawker married to Gertrude, he lived in Beeston Road, Sheringham. Enlisted in 1st Battalion Essex Regiment, died (aged 36) on 13th April 1917 at the First Battle of Scarpe, which was considered to have been a great success for the British. He has no known grave and is commemorated on the Arras Memorial, Pas de Calais.

HORACE CREASEY

Born in Framfield, Sussex in 1818, and employed as a gardener, he lived with his wife Ellen and family in Priory Road, Sheringham. He enlisted in 1st Battalion of the Norfolk Regiment in Norwich. He was killed in action, aged 36, at the Second Battle of Passchendaele, the final phase of the Third Battle of Ypres. He has no known grave and is commemorated on the Tyne Cot Memorial, Zonnebeke, Belgium. His parents, Henry and Louisa Creasey, lost all four of their sons during the war.

BERTIE C DENNIS

Born in Erpingham in 1893, he lived in Sheringhan and was employed as a baker. He joined the 12th Siege Battery of the Royal Garrison Artillery. He died in action on 28th October 1917, aged 24, and is buried in Thelus Military cemetery,

HENRY (HARRY) COLLINGS

© Commonwealth War Graves Commission

Harry, as he was known, was the son of Edward and Rosetta Collings and lived with his parents at The Clyffe, Sheringham, in what is now (in a much sadder state) the Shannocks Hotel.

In 1917 he was a stoker first class on *HMS Cheerful*, a Royal Navy Destroyer.

On 30th June 1917, *HMS Cheerful* struck a mine, laid by a German submarine (*UC-33 Martin Schelle*), off the Shetland Islands. Harry, aged just 16, was among 40 of the crew of 58, who were killed. He has no known grave and is commemorated on Chatham Naval Memorial, Kent. He was the youngest Sheringham casualty.

We are grateful to Margaret Larner, for sharing information and pictures of her great uncle with us.

Pas de Calais. He had been married to his wife Ellen for just ten months.

GEORGE R DENNIS, M.M.

Born in Sheringham in 1888, lived in Beeston Road, Sheringham and was a butcher's assistant. He enlisted in 1st Battalion Cambridgeshire in Braintree Essex. Killed in action (aged 29) on 26th September 1917 at Tower Hamlets Ridge, where there was a German strongpoint known as Joist Redoubt. He was awarded the Military Medal and is buried in Perth Cemetery (China Wall), Ieper, Belgium. He left a wife and young daughter.

ALFRED E ELLIS

Born on 14th January 1881, he was a carpenter and joiner, who lived with his mother. He died at home of tuberculosis on 23rd June 1917, aged 36 years, and is buried in the graveyard at All Saints Church Upper Sheringham.

ROBERT W FIELDS

Born in 1891 in Sheringham, his father was James Fields of Almer House, Beeston Road, Sheringham. He was a professional soldier, who enlisted in Cromer in 1st Battalion Border Regiment, and attained the rank of sergeant. Died of his wounds 30th June 1917, aged 26, in Battle of Scarpe. Buried in Mendinghem Military Cemetery, Poperinge, West-Vlaanderen, Belgium. Robert was one of 17 children sired by his father, the youngest being born when his father was 72!

WILLIAM A FIELDS

Born in Sheringham in 1898, he was a member of the Sheringham Salvation Army band. Aged 17, he enlisted in 8th Battalion Norfolk Regiment in Cromer on 17th November 1915. He died on 25th April 1917, aged 19 years, in the battle of Arras. He is buried in Maroc British Cemetery, Nord, France.

CECIL FOX

Born on 27th April 1896, according to the 1911 census, and lived with his parents at 5 Wellington Terrace, Cromer Road, Sheringham. He worked as a golf caddy and enlisted at Dereham in the 5th Battalion of the Norfolk Regiment. He died in action in Palestine on 15th December 1917, aged 21. He is buried in Ramleh War Cemetery, Israel.

ERNELY HOLSEY

Apparently a resident of Sheringham born in October 1893, he worked as a golf caddy. He enlisted in 1st Battalion of the Essex Regiment. He was killed in action, aged 24 years, at Monchy le Peux in the First Battle of the Scarpe, in the Second Battle of Arras. At 5.30 am that day the 1st Battalion attacked the German lines and he was one of 661 men killed. He has no known grave and is commemorated on the Arras Memorial, Pas de Calais.

RICHARD HOUGHTON

Born in in Huntingdonshire in 1880, he was a sewing machine salesman who lived with his wife in Sheringham. He became a corporal in the Royal Engineers. He died died serving at the RE Signals Depot at Dunstable on 10th April 1917 and was buried in All Saints Churchyard, Upper Sheringham.

GEORGE W KNIGHTS

Born in 1897, the son of Thomas Elisha Knights (cab driver) and Emily Knights. He lived with his parents in Sheringham and worked as an assistant chemist. He enlisted in the 2/4th Battalion of the Leicestershire Regiment at Leicester and reached the rank of lance corporal. He was killed in action on 26th September 1917, aged 21 years, at Polygon Woods. Michael Canty, whose name also appears on the Sheringham War Memorial was a lodger with the Knights family.

REGGIE BULLEN

Thomas Henry Reginald Bullen (Reggie), was born in Fakenham in 1898. He was a lance corporal who, like his brother, served in the 9th Battalion of the Norfolks. In March 1918, the 9th were part of the 6th Division of the British Army at Lagnicourt Sector in Pas de Calais.

Here, No Man's Land averaged three-quarters of a mile in width. A Short History of the 6th Division states that on 21st March 1918: *"A large portion of the front line – notably the valleys – was sown with 2-in. trench-mortar bombs with instantaneous fuses, which would detonate under the pressure of a wagon but not of a man's foot. In addition five anti-tank 18-pounder guns were placed in positions of vantage. The wire was very broad and thick. The position would, indeed, have been almost impregnable had there been sufficient time to complete it, and had there been separate troops for counter-attack."*

The Allied forces learned from German deserters that they were to be heavily attacked. The morning of March 21st 1918 was shrouded in fog as the Germans launched its 'Michael' offensive. The scale of the bombardment by the Germans left no doubt that a massive offensive was underway.

The bombardment, which included gas, continued for five hours. At 8 am, the 9th Norfolks were occupying trenches at the

Arras Memorial

Lagnicourt Switch. By 5.35 pm the whole sector was under intense pressure and the brigade they were in fell back to the Vaulx-Morchies Line. When darkness fell, the remnants of the battalion numbered just 120 men. The night was quiet, as both sides prepared for the next day's struggle. Reggie Bullen was not among the survivors though.

At some time on 21st March 1918, Reggie met his death. On the morning of 23rd March, the whole brigade could muster no more than 290 men from an initial trench strength of 1,800. Like his brother Thereas, Reggie has no known grave. He is commemorated on the Arras Memorial, Pas de Calais.

Little wonder then, that thereafter, Caroline Bullen considered herself a 'sorrowing mother'.

WILLIAM F MACDONALD

Born on 7th July 1894, he was the son of W T Macdonald (a golf professional) and his wife Minnie. He had been an apprentice iron turner in Dundee. He was a second lieutenant in the Royal Field Artillery and was killed in action near Gouzeaucourt on 23rd November 1917, aged 23. His is buried in Gouzeaucourt New British Cemetery, Nord, France

HAROLD H ROGERS

Born in Attleborough around 1898, the son of Charles and Mary Rogers, of Hillbrook, Beeston Common, Sheringham. He worked as a railway clerk and enlisted in Cromer with Princess Louise's (Argyll & Sutherland Highlanders). Died of wounds on 26th April 1917, aged 19. Buried in Mont Huon Military Cemetery, Le Treport, Seine-Maritime, France.

GODFREY B COOK

Godfrey was born at 'Snelsmore Lodge', Winterbourne, Berkshire on 1st December 1894. By 1901 the family were living at 'Hilbre', Holway Road, Sheringham. His father, Arthur Burton Cook, had been born and brought up in Birkenhead, but is not shown as having an occupation. His mother Alice cared for their three children, Godfrey, Clara and Edith, assisted by a cook and two servants.

In 1911 Arthur described himself as living from 'private means'. At this point Godfrey was a boarder at Malvern College. After leaving school he went briefly to Vancouver in Canada to farm but, at the outbreak of war, he returned to England and enlisted as a Trooper in the County of London Yeomanry. He saw action in Egypt and Gallipoli where, on 22nd August 1915, he was severely wounded in the thigh. He was evacuated back to England and admitted to the 5th Northern General Hospital in Leicester.

Later he received a commission in the 20th Hussars as a lieutenant, and served with them for 18 months in France. The exact circumstances surrounding Godfrey's death are uncertain. The battalion war diary records him as having been killed in action on 23rd March (aged 23), but it transpires, from a later communication from the Military Secretary to his father, that he had been badly wounded and *"lying as if dead when he was found by the Germans."* His death was reported by an ambulance company as being the result of "gas poisoning".

He was buried in St Souplet British Cemetery, Nord, France. His parents erected a panel in All Saints Church, Beeston Regis in his memory. It is the centrepiece of the church's Chapel of Remembrance (pictured below).

© Iain Turner

CHARLES P SADLER

Born in Sheringham, the son of Simon and Susan Sadler, he was a bricklayer's labourer. Enlisted in London with No. 6 Army Tramway Company, Royal Engineers. Died of wounds (circumstances unknown) on 4th July 1917, aged 30. Buried in Mendinghem Military Cemetery, Poperinge, West-Vlaanderen, Belgium.

HARRY SMITH

Private 200728, 1st/4th Battalion, Norfolk Regiment. Killed in action on 19th April 1917. Harry Smith was born in Upper Sheringham in 1883. His father was a bricklayer. Harry enlisted in the 1st/4th Battalion, the Norfolk Regiment in 1917. The Second Battle of Gaza began on 19th April 1917 and it was here that Harry was killed in action, aged 34 years. Joseph Tee (the landlord of 'The Lobster') and Reginald Turner (who lived on

Gun Street) were killed in the same battle. Harry is buried in the Gaza War Cemetery.

JOSEPH TEE

Born in Peterborough in July 1882, he was the landlord of 'The Lobster' in Sheringham. He enlisted in Cromer with 1/5th Battalion, Norfolk Regiment. Killed in action in the 2nd Battle of Gaza on 19th April 1917, aged 35. No known grave. Commemorated on Jerusalem Memorial, Israel.

ALBERT E TOOLEY

Born on 2nd November 1885, the son of Isaac Charles and Charlotte Tooley from Belaugh near Wroxham. Married Violet Laura Dunn on 31 July 1911 in Sheringham and described his place of residence as Sheringham. His occupation was recorded as a gardener. They had one son, Jack Edward Tooley, who was born on 1st July 1916 in Sheringham. Albert's occupation was recorded on his son's birth certificate as a lance corporal in the

EDWARD LONG

Edward Long lived with his wife and children in Sheringham. He enlisted in the Norfolk Regiment at the start of the conflict in 1914. He spent much of his army life as a sergeant, training new recruits.

In 1918, saddened by the thought that he had trained so many young men who ended up being killed in action, he applied to his senior officers to be allowed to go to the Front himself. His request was refused, so

he transferred to the 20th Battalion of the Durham Light Infantry.

It was as a member of the Durhams that, on 4th September 1918 (aged 32), he was killed in action, a little more than two months before the end of hostilities. He is buried in Grootebeek British Cemetery, West Vlaanderen, Belgium.

We are grateful to Edward and Peter Long, for sharing about their grandfather.

Sergeant Edward Long (far right)

Suffolk Yeomanry. He died from a fever in Egypt on 17th October 1918. He is buried in Damascus Commonwealth War Cemetery, Egypt.

REGINALD A TURNER

The son of Mrs Ellene Turner of 'Hazelbank', Beeston End, Sheringham. He enlisted in the 1st/5th Battalion, Norfolk Regiment. He was killed in action in the 2nd Battle of Gaza on 19th April 1917, aged 19. No known grave, he is commemorated on the Jerusalem Memorial, Israel. He left a widowed mother and sister.

ROBERT C WEST

Born on 4th January 1884, the son of Henry and Susan West, he was a fisherman and the Salvation Army Bandmaster. He joined the Royal Naval Reserve, as a deck hand on board *HMPMS Queen of the North*, which was formerly a Blackpool Paddle Steamer and was fitted out as a minesweeper based at Harwich. He was killed on 20th July 1917, aged 23 years, when the boat struck a mine off Orford Ness and sank with the loss of 29 men. No known grave, he is commemorated on Chatham Naval Memorial.

WILLIAM W WEST

Born in, and resident of, Sheringham, he was a labourer. He initially joined the Norfolk Regiment, but ended up as a private 21257, 6th Battalion, Border Regiment. He died of his wounds on 27th August 1917, aged 32, following action at Ypres. He is buried in Dozinghem, Military Cemetery, Poperinge, West-Vlaanderen, Belgium.

BERTIE WHITE

Born in Briston, Norfolk, enlisted in Cromer with 12th Battalion, Royal Sussex Regiment. Killed in action during attacks to take the 'Fifteen Ravine' on 25th September 1917, aged 19. He was buried in a row of 15 men, only two of whom

have been identified. He has no known grave and is commemorated on the Tyne Cot Memorial, Zonnebeke, Belgium.

HARRY WILSON

Born in 1886 in Exmouth, the son of Denny and Maria Wilson. In the 1911 census he was living with his parents at 1 Scarborough Villas, Mill Lane, Sheringham, along with his wife Pertha. He was working as a carpenter/builder. Subsequently he and his wife emigrated to Australia. Harry enlisted in 3/51st Battalion, Australian Infantry. He was killed on 2nd April 1917 in the attack on Noreuil. His body was not recovered and he is commemorated on the Villers-Bretonneux Australian Memorial on the Somme.

CHRISTOPHER WOODHOUSE

Born in Sheringham on 2nd May 1892, he was the son of William and Caroline Woodhouse, and worked as a general labourer. Enlisted in Norwich and was a private in 1st Battalion, Cambridgeshire Regiment. Killed in action near Hill Top Farm on 27th May 1917, aged 25. He left a widow, Eliza. Buried in Vlamertinghe Military Cemetery, Ieper, West-Vlaanderen, Belgium.

1918

ARTHUR C BIRD

Born in West Beckham in 1888. In 1911, he was a butcher in Mortlake, Surrey. In 1918, he was living with his wife at Manor Farm, West Beckham – now 'The Wheatsheaf'. Enlisted in Cromer with the Advanced Motor Transport Depot, Royal Army Service Corps. He died of burns in Mesopotamia on 5th May 1918, aged 30. Buried in Baghdad (North Gate) War Cemetery, Iraq.

WILLIAM B BISHOP

Born in Sheringham in 1891, the son of John Robert and Emma Augusta Bishop. He was a fisherman, as was his father. He married his wife Florence and lived at Ashton House, Cremer Street, Sheringham. He enlisted in Norwich with

MERVYN H W TRENDELL

Mervyn Trendell was born on 8th July 1899 in Sprowston and, on 5th August, was baptised (probably by his father). In 1901, the family lived in the Vicarage in Sprowston. Mervyn's father, George, was the vicar and his mother, Alexandria, looked after her four children with the aid of three servants. Gwendoline (11) was the eldest child, followed by Claude (8), Cuthbert (3) and Mervyn (1).

By 1911, the family had moved to Sheringham and lived at the Vicarage, Vicarage Road (now the 'Old Vicarage'). Claude had left home at this stage. It is possible he was either away at school or studying at university. When the family first moved to Sheringham, Mervyn attended Mr Underhill's School and then, in May 1913, he moved to Gresham's School in Holt.

He was there for three years, leaving after the Easter term of 1917 and going straight to the Royal Aircraft Factory at Farnborough, where he remained – working through the various shops – until the following July. He passed the examinations for probationary flying officer in the Royal Naval Air Service and was taught to fly. He was commissioned in February 1918 and posted to *HMS Galatea*, a battle cruiser patrolling the North Sea off Scotland.

At 16.43 hours on 18th May 1918, he took off from his ship to carry signals to the RNAS station at Donibristle in Fife. He was flying a Sopwith Camel 2F.1 (serial number N6766). On its final approach to the airfield, Mervyn's plane clipped a tree and crashed. Suffering severe injuries, he was immediately shipped across the Firth of Forth to the Royal Naval Hospital at South Queensferry. He succumbed to his injuries the next day, Whit Sunday 1918, aged 18. His parents received the news of his accident and of his death that day.

The newspaper report notes *"...coming so soon after the news and uncertainty about the whereabouts and condition of their second son, who is a prisoner in Germany, this blow is all the more felt by the bereaved parents and family..."*

His body was brought home and interred in his father's churchyard at Upper Sheringham with full military honours.

Inland Water Transport, Royal Engineers. He died at home of stomach cancer on 24th January 1918, aged 28. He is buried in All Saints Churchyard, Upper Sheringham.

MICHAEL CANTY

He was born in Kilkee, Co. Clare, Ireland in 1883. In the 1911 census, he was a lodger with George W Knight's family in Sheringham, and his occupation was given as painter/builder. He enlisted in the 8th Battalion, Rifle Brigade (The Prince Consort's Own) and was killed in action during the 'Pursuit to Mons' on 3rd November 1918 (eight days before the Armistice was signed), aged 35. He is buried in Terlincthun British Cemetery, Wimille, Pas de Calais, France.

BERTIE J COOPER

Born in Norwich in 1899, the son of Benjamin and Annie Cooper. His father was a fruiterer on Station Road, Sheringham. Enlisted in 1st Battalion, Queen's Own (Royal West Kent) Regiment. He was killed in action near the Canal du Nord on 27th September 1918, aged 19. Buried in Gouzeaucourt, New British Cemetery, Nord, France.

Your King and Country Thank You.

HOME WORDS NO. 168

Christmas Greetings from   to

Christmas greetings from the Front

GEORGE DAY

Private in the 2nd Battalion, the Suffolk Regiment. Died of wounds received during the 'Hundred Days Offensive' on 16th June 1918, aged 24. He left a widow, Elsie.

WILLIAM B DENNIS

Born in Upper Sheringham in 1883, he was a housepainter. Enlisted in Cromer and ended up with 10th Battalion, Essex Regiment. He was killed in action near Epehy on 21st September 1918, aged 36. Buried in Unicorn Cemetery, Vend'huille, Aisne, France.

FREDERICK DUFFIELD

Born on 13th November 1897, the son of Charles and Anna Duffield, of Beeston Common, Sheringham. His father was a general labourer. Frederick enlisted in Dereham with 1st/4th Battalion, Duke of Wellington's (West Riding Regiment). He died of wounds received near

Reutel on 13th March 1918, aged 20. He was buried in Menin Road South Military Cemetery, Ieper, West-Vlaanderen, Belgium.

JOHN H DUMBLE

Born at Sheringham in January 1888, he was the son of William and Amelia Dumble from the town. His father died in 1908. John was a golf club maker. He enlisted in Oakham, Rutlandshire, with 7th Battalion, Leicestershire Regiment, whilst resident in Stamford, Lincolnshire. He died of wounds received during the Battle of the Aisne on 29th May 1918, aged 30. He left a widow. He is buried in Rethel French National Cemetery, Ardennes, France.

HAROLD E HARTT

Born in October 1890 in Beckenham, Kent, the son of Charles Hartt and Blanche May Hartt (both died 1893). He was an advertising canvasser and lived at 'Claremont', Holway Road, Sheringham. Enlisted at Hornsey with D Company, 1st/5th

Battalion, London Regiment (London Rifle Brigade). He was killed in action on the first day of the Battle of Arras on 28th March 1918, aged 27. He has no known grave and is commemorated on Arras Memorial, Pas de Calais, France.

GEORGE HAWKSLEY

Born in 1890 in Lincoln, he was the son of George and Florence Hawkesly. In 1911, he was an articled estate agent, who played hockey for North Norfolk. He enlisted in the Royal Inniskilling Fusiliers, as a lieutenant. He died of wounds received defending against the German Spring Offensive on 22nd March 1918, aged 28. He left a widow, Ethel, and is buried in Bronfay Farm Military Cemetery, Bray-sur-Somme, Somme, France.

GORDON C LOADES

Born in 1898 , son of William and Emily Loades of 'Brookside', The Avenue, Sheringham. He won a scholarship to Paston Grammar School. He enlisted in the 13th Battalion, Royal Sussex Regiment, and was captured by the Germans and held as a prisoner of war. He died in captivity from disease on 31st October 1918, aged 20. He was buried in the Ohlsdorfer Friedhof cemetery, Ohlsdorf, Hamburg-Nord, Hamburg, Germany.

RICHARD A MACK, M.M.

Born in 1894 in Sheringham, the son of Richard and Florence Mack, he was a delivery boy. He enlisted in the 7th Battalion, Norfolk Regiment. He was a corporal, who died of wounds received during the advance through Artois on 7th October 1918, aged 24. He is buried in St Sever Cemetery Extension, Rouen, Seine-Maritime, France. He was awarded the Military Medal (M.M.).

THOMAS MORRIS

Born on 6 May 1862 in Upwey, Weymouth, Dorset. He was the husband of Lavinia Morris, of Ivy Cottage, West Cliff, Sheringham. He was Chief Petty Officer at the Coastguard Station (Sheringham) and died of heart disease on 6th February 1918, aged 56. His son, Walter, was evacuated from the Somme and died in 1916. Father and son are buried beside each other at All Saints Churchyard, Upper Sheringham.

CHARLES E PEGG

Born on 3rd July 1900, he was the son of Frederick and Martha Pegg. He enlisted in the 10th Battalion, Rifle Brigade (The Prince Consort's Own). He died on 27th October 1918 in Northampton, aged 18, whilst serving with 53rd Y.S. Battalion, Rifle Brigade. He is buried in All Saints Churchyard, Upper Sheringham.

ALBERT E TOOLEY

Born on 2nd November 1885, nothing is known of his parents. He was a gardener and married his wife Violet in July 1911. He enlisted in Ely with the Household Cavalry and died from a fever in Egypt on 17th October 1918, aged 27.

RALPH E WINN

Born in Kington-on-Thames on 25th October 1891. He was the son of William and Agatha Winn, of Beach Villa, Cliff Road, Sheringham. He was an organ builder by trade. He enlisted in Rochdale with 1st Battalion, Queen's (Royal West Surrey Regiment) and was killed in action on 11th January 1918, aged 26. He has no known grave and is commemorated on Tyne Cott Memorial, Zonnebeke, West-Vlaanderen, Belgium.

Reconstruction of a WWI bunker at Sheringham Museum

1919

ALBERT G BUMFREY LEE

Born on 25th August 1889 in Bessingham, Norfolk, he was the son of Albert and Sarah Bumfrey. He worked as a carter and married his wife Catherine in February 1913. He enlisted in the Royal Army Service Corps and contracted malaria whilst serving in Salonika. He is recorded as dying of Spanish Flu and malaria at home in Sheringham, aged 30, in Autumn 1919.

BEESTON REGIS WAR MEMORIAL

Below are the names of those who gave their lives during World War One and are commemorated on Beeston Regis Memorial, All Saints Church Beeston Regis:

Frederick J APPLEGATE
Walter W COOPER
Frederick DUFFIELD
Sidney DYBALL
Edward LONG
Frederick A MORTIMER
Harold H ROGERS
Frederick E TURNEY
James J TURNEY

Further details are included among those listed on the Sheringham Memorial. In addition, the following two men are commemorated on both the memorials at Beeston Regis and at West Runton.

1916

ERNEST F HORNE

Born on 19th March, 1894 in West Runton, son of Arthur and Alice Horne of Herne House. Enlisted on 12th May 1915 in London as able seaman Z/1782, Royal Naval Volunteer Reserve. Died on 13th November 1916 at the battle of the Ancre, the final phase of the Battle of the Somme. He was one of 2,469 casualties. Commemorated at Ancre British Cemetery, Beaumont-Hamel, France.

1918

ROBERT W KING

Born in 1895 in Roydon, Norfolk, son of Robert and Edith King of 'Glengarriff', West Runton. Second lieutenant in 1st Battalion Cambridgeshire Regiment. Killed in action on 27th March 1918. One of 14,655 UK casualties who died on the Somme battlefields between 21 March 1918 and 7 August 1918 and who are commemorated on the Pozieres Memorial, Ovillers-la-Boisselle, France.

War Savings Certificate advertisement on paper bag

Dedication of Upper Sheringham War Memorial

UPPER SHERINGHAM WAR MEMORIAL

Below are the names of those who gave their lives during World War One, as recorded on the Upper Sheringham War Memorial.

Researched and compiled by Simon Bottomley of Upper Sheringham and assisted by Gary Hughes, Upper Sheringham Parish Councillor

1915

HAROLD R DUNT

Born in Upper Sheringham, son of William and Louisa Mary Dunt, of The Gardens, Sheringham Hall, Upper Sheringham and the brother of Sydney Charles Dunt, who died five days before him. A private in 7th Battalion of the Norfolk Regiment, died (aged 18) of wounds received during the Third Battle of Artois on 17th October 1915. One of 61,000 British casualties in the battle, he is buried in Abbeville Communal Cemetery in the Somme.

SYDNEY C DUNT

Like his brother above, he was the son of William and Louisa Mary Dunt of The Gardens, Sheringham Hall, Sheringham and was also a private in 7th Battalion of the Norfolk Regiment. Sydney was killed in action (aged 21), again during the Third Battle of Artois on 17th October 1915, another of the 61,000 British casualties. He has no known grave, but is commemorated on Loos Memorial, Pas de Calais, France.

1916

FREDRICK B DEW

Frederick was the son of Mr B Dew of Baconsthorpe and husband of Brenda M Dew and lived and worked at Sheringham Hall. He was a lance corporal in the 2nd Battalion, Norfolk Regiment and was killed in action (aged 23) on 23rd March 1916 during the Siege of Kut-el-Amara, in Mesopotamia. He has no known grave but is commemorated on the Basra Memorial, Iraq.

GERALD T WHALL

Born in Sheringham, a private in the 2nd Battalion, Norfolk Regiment. He died on 31st July 1916, aged 17, during the Mesopotamia campaign. This lasted from November 1914 to November 1918, where British and Indian troops fought against the Ottoman Turks in Mesopotamia (now Iraq). During the campaign, the British and their allies suffered over 85,000 battle casualties. Many more men were hospitalised for non-battle causes, like sickness, with nearly 17,000 men dying from disease. Gerald was one of those and has no known grave, but, like Fredrick Dew, he is commemorated on the Basra Memorial, Iraq.

1917

EDWIN (EDWYN) HARMER

Born in 1892, the son of Robert and Elizabeth Harmer, of Park Lodge, Upper Sheringham. A private in the 1st/5th Battalion (Territorial), Norfolk Regiment, he enlisted in Cromer and died (aged 25) in Palestine on 19th April 1917. He has no known grave but is commemorated on the Jerusalem Memorial, Israel.

JOHN H HOWELL

Born in Sheringham, he enlisted in Cromer, as a private in the 1st/4th Battalion of the Norfolk Regiment, part of the Norfolk & Suffolk Brigade of the East Anglian Division. He was one of 1,071 killed in action on 25th September 2017, in the Battle of the Menin Road Ridge, during the Third Battle of Ypres (aged 21). He is buried in Tyne Cott Cemetery, Zonnebeck, West-Vlaaneren, Belgium.

1918

ROBERT W PEGG

Born in 1900, Robert was the son of Mrs Jemima Ann Pegg of 50 Park Road, Upper Sheringham. He enlisted in Bury St Edmunds in the 53rd Battalion, Bedfordshire Regiment, but died in the United Kingdom of pneumonia, aged 18, on 1st November 1918. He was one of 30,000 from his regiment who gave their lives in World War One

and is buried in All Saints Churchyard, Upper Sheringham.

ROBERT H PURDY

Born in Sheringham, he was the son of Robert and Hannah Purdy of Upper Sheringham. He enlisted in Norwich as a private in the 1st/4th Battalion, Norfolk Regiment and died of his wounds in Palestine (aged 29) on 4th January 1918. He is buried in Kantara War Memorial Cemetery, Egypt.

CHARLES F NUNNELEY

Born 31st December 1883, at Rennington in Northumberland. He married Hon. Edith Marjery Mansfield, the daughter of John William Mansfield 3rd Baron Sandhurst on 12th October 1910. At least from 1904 to 1924, Lord Sandhurst lived at Edgebrook, Holway Road, Sheringham. He was a practising barrister and was a local magistrate for many years.

Edgebrook, in those days, was a 26 room mansion and in the 1911 census, Lord Sandhurst had at least seven resident servants. In that same census, Charles Francis Nunneley is listed as the son-in-law of the head of the household. He was also an active member of Sheringham Golf Club.

In The Great War he re-joined the Northumberland Fusiliers in August 1914 and was killed in action on 26 October 1914 (aged 30) at Neuve Chapelle on the Western Front. He was mentioned in dispatches, when his Commanding Officer wrote: *"The enemy had captured a trench in which was a gun. He attempted to recapture the trench by crawling through a wire fence, which was about thirty yards from the enemy. His men got hung up in the wire, and Lieutenant Nunneley calmly stood up, encouraging and directing them regardless of all personal risks, and was shot at close quarters by the enemy."*

WORLD WAR ONE IN NUMBERS

LOCAL

PARISHES OF SHERINGHAM, BEESTON REGIS AND UPPER

- The First World War left 21 Sheringham women widowed.

- 20 sons and 15 daughters were left without a father.

- 11 of those who died had not yet reached their 20th birthday.

- 11 of those who died were older than 35.

- The youngest casualty was just 16 years old.

- The oldest was 56.

- Of the 82 who died, 10 died from disease.

NATIONAL

- Many British recruits were undernourished and put on over a stone in weight with good food and exercise.

- In 1914, a private earned a shilling a day.

- 80,000 British soldiers suffered from shellshock during the war.

- By the end of the war there were 250,000 men who had suffered full or partial amputation.

- If all those who died (soldiers and civilians) held hands, the line would stretch beyond Australia.

- It would take 625 days to read out a list of christian names and surnames of those who gave their lives.

INTERNATIONAL

- 70% of all battle casualties were caused by artillery.

- A total of 1.2 million men were lost during the Battle of the Somme. The furthest the allies advanced was 7.8 miles.

- During the 4 years of the war, there were 6.6 million civilian deaths – 2 million in Russia alone.

- 8 million soldiers died – 6,000 for each day of the war or 250 every hour.

- 21.2 million men were wounded.

- 5 out of every 9 men sent to France became a casualty.

- The Thiepval Memorial alone has the names of 72,116 men with no known grave.

Compiled by Iain Turner

THE ARDLEY BROTHERS: THREE CONSCIENTIOUS OBJECTORS

Many towns had conscientious objectors. Often ostracised by their fellow residents who had sons, husbands and brothers fighting at the Front, a large number of these men had religious reasons for refusing to fight but still wanted to 'do their bit' for King and Country and their fellow man. Thus, they often became Red Cross workers – orderlies, ambulance drivers and stretcher bearers – very dangerous, harrowing and brave occupations.

The Ardley brothers were three brothers whose family were well known Quakers in the area. Their father, James, had a shop in town (currently the site of WH Smith near the clock tower). All three were given absolute exemption from military fighting on the grounds of conscientious objection.

Very little is known of the brothers but basic research reveals they were all attached to the Red Cross, Friends Ambulance Unit and Order of St John ambulance units in France.

Cards like this ridiculed men who became conscientious objectors

ALAN FREDERICK ARDLEY (BORN 1896)

Alan is listed as an apprentice bookseller on his Red Cross record. He is single, as are all the brothers.

His period of service began on 18th September 1915 in the rank of orderly. He became an ambulance driver in 1916 and continued until his date of termination on 17th February 1919.

Mr Ardley senior in front of his shop

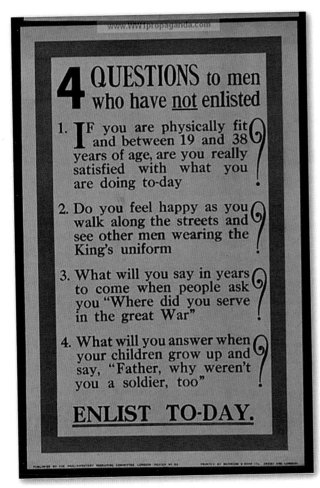

Enlist... what are you waiting for?

He was awarded the Croix de Guerre by the French government in August 1918 for services to the SSA (Section Sanitaire Anglaise) 14 convoy to which he was attached.

After the war, Alan married Mary Paisley in 1936, aged 40, and lived in Cumbria. On the 1939 census he is listed as a clerk. He died in 1978, aged 82.

BASIL ARDLEY (BORN 1894)

Basil is listed as an electrician on his service card. His period of service began in France on 22nd February 1915 in the rank of orderly. He was then listed as a driver and was also attached to the SSA 14.

He continued to work for the SSA 14 until 31st January 1919 and was awarded the Croix de Guerre at the same time as his brother, Alan.

After the war, Basil remained single and died in 1986 in Sheringham at the age of 92. He had been living with his sister, Mary. On the 1939 census his profession is listed as assembler of scientific instruments.

FRANCIS JOHN ARDLEY (BORN 1888)

Francis is listed as single and a grocer living at Lynton House, Church Street, Sheringham (the same address is given for all three Ardley boys).

His date of engagement in the war began on 30th January 1915. He soon became a cook and then a driver with the SSA 14. He continued to work with the unit until his termination on 29th December 1918.

There is no record of Francis receiving the Croix de Guerre. He died in 1935, at the age of 47, still living at Lynton House, Sheringham,

All three were awarded the British War Medal, Victory Medal and the 14-15 Star.

Researched and compiled by Jane Crossen

Proud proclamation of a relative at war

WAS IT WORTH IT?

A reflection by Peter Farley

"Strange friend," I said, "here is no cause to mourn."
"None," said that other, "save the undone years,
The hopelessness. Whatever hope is yours,
Was my life also; ...

"For by my glee might many men have laughed,
And of my weeping something had been left,
Which must die now. I mean the truth untold,
The pity of war, the pity war distilled.
Now men will go content with what we spoiled.
Or, discontent, boil bloody, and be spilled."

The above extract is from *Strange Meeting* by Wilfred Owen. Owen was fatally wounded just a week before the war ended. Apparently, suffering from shell shock, he was anxious to return to the Front, as a means of justifying his art. Just before his death, writing to his brother, he said: *"I know I shall be killed, but it's the only place I can make my protest from."*

COST BENEFIT ANALYSIS

If it were possible to carry out a cost benefit analysis of World War One, what would it reveal? The more you read and hear about the conflict the more futile it can seem. The photo below, like so many of its kind, begs the question – was it worth it?

This photograph, taken by an Australian official photographer on 12 October 1917, shows a captured German blockhouse near the ruins of

Commonwealth of Australia (Department of Veterans' Affairs)

Zonnebeke railway station, not far from Tyne Cot (above), site of the world's largest allied cemetery.

For me, the following extract from Martyn Barr's book, *'The Lost Generation'*, is a very graphic rendering of the question:

THE THIRD BATTLE OF YPRES (PASSCHENDAELE)

The British were further encouraged by the success of an attack on the Messines Ridge on 7 June 1917. Nineteen huge mines were exploded simultaneously after they had been placed at the end of long tunnels under the German front line. General Haig decided to launch a third offensive at Ypres, with the aim of securing the high ground around the village of Passchendaele. His ultimate goal was once again to destroy the German U-boat bases along the Belgian coast, which were still posing a major threat to British supply ships.

British artillery bombarded the German lines at Passchendaele for ten days. Three thousand artillery guns fired over four million shells, turning the battlefield into an impenetrable quagmire.

Pre-warned by the heavy bombardment, the Germans were fully prepared for an Allied attack and the British made little headway. Then, in early August, the area was saturated with the heaviest rain the region had seen in 30 years. The offensive descended into chaos, as British supply vehicles, tanks and heavy artillery sank into the thick mud. Wooden tracks were laid down for the soldiers to walk across, but thousands of men and horses drowned in the sea of mud.

During the battle, the Germans unleashed a fearsome new weapon on the Allied troops – mustard gas – one of the most lethal of all the poisonous chemicals used during the First World War. It had virtually no smell and took 12 hours to take effect, so soldiers were not aware they had received a deadly dose until it was too late. Mustard gas burnt the skin, eyes, windpipe and lungs. Affected soldiers could suffer a long and painful death.

After months of carnage, British and Canadian troops finally took Passchendaele village in November 1917. But the victory was short lived. Within weeks, the Germans had recaptured all their lost ground and the U-boats remained free to roam the seas. Both sides paid a high price for the failure of the offensive: Allied casualties numbered around 325,000 men and the Germans around 260,000.

To my mind, 585,000 men killed (325,000 Allied casualties and 260,000 German) was most certainly not worth it. So great a cost in lives, for so little benefit in terms of ground won (only to be lost a few weeks later), can never be justified.

THE SURVIVORS

The following are the stories of some of those who returned home, as told by Iain Turner

ARCHIE THOMAS PAGE (1891 – 1948)

Archie Thomas Page was born in 1891 in Framlingham in Suffolk, the youngest son of John and Sarah. John had trained as a plumber, but the family were living at the Castle Brewery where he was a brewer.

Archie was the youngest of four siblings. The 1901 census shows his sister Henrietta was 23 and his other sister, Beatrice, was 21. His older brother Herbert was 18 and an 'ironmonger's apprentice'. Archie was 9 and at school. John's younger brother, George, lived with the family and worked as a 'brewer's clerk'.

Archie attended Framlingham College from 1901 until 1908. In 1905, he won the Goldsmith Prize and Silver Medal for Modern Languages.

By 1911, Archie had left home and moved to Peterborough. He lived on the High Street with his brother Herbert who was an 'ironmonger'. Archie was his assistant.

The spirit of adventure shone in young Archie, however, and in 1913 he emigrated to South America aged only 21. On 22nd February 1913, he left Liverpool on the Argentinian ship *El Paraguayo* bound for Buenos Aires. The vessel, commanded by Ship's Master C S Crichton, was not a particularly large one and carried only five passengers. Archie declared himself to be a 'poultryman' and indicated his intention to remain in Argentina permanently.

However, his son Eddie says that when he heard of the outbreak of war, he immediately set sail for the UK and joined the Suffolk Regiment. As he did not go to France until October 1915, it is likely that he did not join up until the early spring of 1915 which would have put him into one of the later battalions to be raised – perhaps the 8th or 9th. His records do not survive and so this must remain pure supposition.

What we do know is that Archie served in one of the six battalions of the Suffolks who played their part in the Battle of the Somme, for it was during this phase of the war that he received the very worst sort of 'blighty' – he lost both feet in action. Like so many young men of his generation, his life was changed forever – and probably shortened considerably – by the war.

In December 1919, he married Ellen Elizabeth Bennett at Plomesgate in Suffolk.

On 15th July 1926, he took the licence for 'The Albion' public house in Thetford. Four years later he took the licence of the 'Eagle Inn' at Tattersett. He later returned to animal husbandry and died, at the very young age of 56, in 1948 – only three years after his father. It is interesting to note that 1948 is a year in which Sheringham lost a number of WW1 veterans. Perhaps 30 years was enough for them?

His son, Eddie, remembers his father *"walking up to the Robin Hood every night for his pint and game of dominoes."* Bearing in mind that he was using prosthetic feet at a very early stage in their development, this demonstrates the determination Archie had to 'soldier on'.

Archie is buried in the churchyard at All Saints Church, Beeston Regis along with Ellen his wife, who died in 1965. The inscription also includes the memory of George Thomas Page, their son, who died as a prisoner of war in Thailand working on the infamous Burma Railway.

FRANK FELMINGHAM (1883 – 1947)

Frank was born in Yarmouth in 1883, the son of John Felmingham and his wife Sarah. John was a labourer for a bricklayer and the young Frank had five siblings. The 1891 census shows his older brother, Arthur, was a ropemaker and his older sister, Bessie, was a domestic servant. Alfred, William and Edith were all at school.

Ten years later, at the age of 18, Frank had left school and was living in Sheringham with the Tice family at 4 Gun Street. The house still stands today and it is difficult to imagine how eight people lived under its small roof. Richard Tice was a bootmaker and his wife, Ellen, looked after their five children and their 18 year old lodger, Frank. The eldest son, James, was a carter and his brother, Arthur, a bootmaker like his father. Nelly, Dorothy and Flossie were still at school. Frank's profession is given simply as 'hairdresser'.

There was obviously a flame of ambition in young Frank because by the 1911 census things had changed somewhat. Frank was now 28 and living with his wife Maude on Co-operative Street in a five room house. They had a boarder, Jonathan Gray, who worked as an 'ironmonger's assistant'. Frank is described as a 'hairdresser – employer'.

He and Maude, who was eight years his elder, married in 1904 at the Wesleyan Chapel in Holt. The same year Maude gave birth to a baby son, Frank, who sadly died soon afterwards. As if one tragedy was not enough, in 1909 she gave birth to Frederick who died less than a year later. On 26th

June 1912, Maude gave birth to a healthy son, William Reginald Felmingham.

Frank's census and voter records show that the family owned (and at times probably lived above) the salon in Co-operative Street. They also had a house, 'Oakdene', on The Avenue. Business was going well for Frank.

Following the passing of new conscription regulations that included married men to the age of 41, Frank was called up. He reported for attestation on 8th June 1916 and, after training, landed in France on 17th July 1917. Initially he served with the 2nd Battalion, Suffolk Regiment before being transferred to the 4th Battalion, the Essex Regiment. He was then transferred to the

2nd Battalion, the Northamptonshire Regiment. On 27th May 1918 he received a serious gunshot wound to his left hip and was evacuated back to England. He was discharged from the Cambridge Hospital in Aldershot in early January and was finally able to return to his family. He was classed as 20% disabled and received a pension of 5/6d a week.

In 1920 Maude gave birth to their daughter Joyce. Frank died on 24th September 1947 aged 64.

ROBERT WILLIAM FUNNELL (1894 – 1970)

Robert Funnell was born on 2nd February 1894 to Robert Oldman Funnell and his wife Margaret Mary (née Taylor). The family lived at 'Chapel of Ease Cottage' in Sheringham which is still owned by his son Robert and his wife Eugenia.

The 1911 census shows Robert to be seventeen years old and a 'cycle mechanic'. His father was the roads foreman for the Council and his younger brother, Jimmy, was a 'news boy'. Young Robert loved all things mechanical and, when he volunteered and took his attestation oath on 4th September 1914, he gave his occupation as 'motor cycle repairer'.

He was initially posted to the Essex Regiment and then transferred on 11th January 1915 to the Royal Field Artillery (Motor Machine Gun Service.) His mechanical skills had been noted. He was posted to France and landed at Boulogne on 7th February 1915, just four months after joining up. Later that year, on 1st December, he was transferred to the Machine Gun Corps, probably to continue the work he had been doing so far.

His record shows that on 12th October 1915 he was *"slightly wounded – still at post"*.

The very first tanks to be used on the battlefield went into action at the Battle of Flers-Courcelette on 15th September 1916. The date of Robert's transfer to tanks is unclear, but he was discharged in March 1919 from 25th Battalion, the Tank Regiment.

What is very clear is that he was awarded the Military Medal on 6th January 1917 in a large British raid on German positions south-east of Arras. Tanks were at the fore and created gaps in the German front line which British troops were able to take advantage of.

On 29th March 1919, Robert was officially demobilised and able to return home to his family. In the 1950s he opened Westcliffe Garage which is still in the family to this day.

He passed away in 1970 at the age of 76.

MARLBOROUGH WALTON PICTON PEGG

In the course of compiling this book we have come across some spectacular happenings but also some hidden nuggets. One of the latter came out of a conversation with Sheringham Town Councillor, Stephen Picton Page. He told us about his grandfather, Marlborough Walter Picton Pegg, who was a Sheringham/Beeston man, one of the local 'Tommies' who served in the Great War.

Stephen recounted that Marlborough was too short for the 'Norfolks' but being determined to enlist, joined the Suffolk Regiment. An unexpected consequence of joining the Suffolks was that, as the shortest man in the regiment, he was introduced to King George V at an inspection!

Whilst at the front, Marlborough was wounded and taken prisoner. He returned to Sheringham after the war and became a market gardener and lived until the 1960s. Marlborough was a very talented musician, being able to play many instruments. He was well-known in the area as a pianist, leading singalongs in the local hostelries. Stephen said his grandfather hardly, if ever, spoke about his experiences.

Within these few paragraphs, we catch the merest glimpse of what so many endured and yet felt unable to share with their nearest and dearest. What was the ripple effect on family and friends? How marred were so many memories and relationships?

SHERINGHAM REMEMBERS

2018 PROGRAMME

Sheringham World War One Centenary
Commemoration and Remembrance Project

PULL-OUT
INSERT

SHERINGHAM REMEMBERS

2018 PROGRAMME

All the individuals, organisations and business involved in the Sheringham World War One Centenary Commemoration and Remembrance Project have, separately and collectively, sought to acknowledge the tremendous debt we owe to all those who lived in the town between 1914 to 1918. In their honour, various events have been arranged throughout November 2018. At the time of going to press, the following are those events we are aware had been planned:

DATE	TIME	VENUE	EVENT	COST & TICKETS
Monday 5 November	**7.30 pm**	St Peter's Church, Sheringham	Talk on *'Ministry on the Front Line - WW1 to Iraq'*	
Wednesday 7 November	**7.30 pm**	Sheringham Little Theatre	Talk on *'Norfolk - the Armistice and After'*	£7 from Box Office 01263 822347
Saturday 10 November	**10 am to 4 pm**	At St Peter's Church Hall, Sheringham Town Hall, North Norfolk Railway Station and Tesco's foyer, there will be static displays of *'Tribute to the Fallen'* figures plus videos, photographs, information and music		
	4.30 pm	There will be an *'Off to war, be home for Christmas, send off'* with a parade of the *'Tribute to the Fallen'* figures on the platform, before they depart on a steam train. For those seeing them off there will be refreshments and music of the time.		
	7.30 pm	Sheringham Little Theatre	Film *Journey's End*	£7 U16s £4 Box Office 01263 822347
		St Peter's Church, Sheringham	*Music for Remembrance* Sheringham and Cromer Choral Society	£12 (£15 on door) U18s free Box Office 01263 822 347

DATE	TIME	VENUE	EVENT	COST & TICKETS
Sunday 11 November	10.45 am	Sheringham War Memorial	Royal British Legion Remembrance Service	
	11 am	All Saints Church, Upper Sheringham	Remembrance Service and dedication of Memorial Plaque followed by a gathering in Village Hall	
	11.15 am	St Peter's Church, Sheringham	Town Remembrance Service	
	5.30 pm	Beeston Hall School, Beeston	Beeston Regis Residents Commemoration Event	Free to Beeston Regis residents (for full details contact Beeston Regis Parish Council)
	7 pm	The Leas, Sheringham	*'Battles Over'* Beacon Lighting Ceremony	
	7.30 pm	Sheringham Little Theatre	Film *Private Peaceful*	£7 U16s £4 Box Office 01263 822347
Monday 12 November	10.30am	St Peter's Church, Sheringham	Sheringham Community Primary School Remembrance Service	
Sunday 18 November	5 pm	St Peter's Church, Sheringham	Poetry Recital	£5 Box Office 01263 822347
Saturday 10 November	10 am to 4 pm	Sheringham Museum	'Lest We Forget' - Sheringham WWI special exhibition	FREE
Sunday 11 November	12 pm to 4 pm	Sheringham Museum	'Lest We Forget' - Sheringham WWI special exhibition	FREE

BATTLE'S OVER

A NATION'S TRIBUTE
11TH NOVEMBER 2018
100 YEARS OF REMEMBRANCE

Battle's Over is a unique series of events in the morning and evening of Sunday 11th November 2018, to mark the day 100 years ago when the guns fell silent at the end of the First World War. Battle's Over is organised by Pageant Master Bruno Peek LVO OBE OPR, a true Norfolk 'Bor', We are very grateful to him for permission to use material from the publicity for this event. Organisations and communities the length and breadth of our nation and in many countries abroad, will play their part in remembering the sacrifice of millions by joining in the Battle's Over tribute.

From the programme inside you will see the events that will be taking place in Sheringham, Beeston Regis and Upper Sheringham. The culmination of these events will be the Beacon Lighting, which takes place at 7 pm on The Leas, Sheringham. At the same time, hundreds of beacons will be lit across the United Kingdom and overseas.

SHERINGHAM AND CROMER CHORAL SOCIETY CENTENARY CONCERT

Sheringham and Cromer Choral Society has been particularly keen to mark the centenary of the First World War over the last four years. To mark the choir's 80th anniversary of choral singing in Sheringham and district, the internationally renowned and locally based composer, Patrick Hawes, was commissioned to write a major new choral piece for choir, orchestra and soprano soloist.

With tremendous support from Arts Council England, Orchestras Live and many others this new work entitled *Eventide (in memoriam Edith Cavell)* was first performed in Norwich Cathedral in July 2014 and received its Sheringham premiere in St Peter's Church, Sheringham during Remembrance weekend in November 2014. Both concerts were accompanied by the English Chamber Orchestra. The libretto very movingly told the story of the last few days of Norfolk nurse, Edith Cavell, executed in Belgium for her part in helping allied soldiers escape from war torn Europe.

The choir will mark the centenary of the Armistice on 11 November 1918 with the

Sheringham Armistice Centenary Concert in St Peter's Church on Saturday 10 November 2018 at 7.30 pm. The concert will feature suitable music for remembrance including Ralph Vaughan Williams' very moving *Dona Nobis Pacem* which he wrote in 1936 pleading for peace by referring to previous wars during the growing fears of a new one. The work includes texts from poems by Walt Whitman and from the book of Jeremiah.

The programme includes Gabriel Fauré's much loved *Requiem* with its focus on eternal rest and consolation. The choir will also perform a short piece called *Christian Soldiers* which is the opening movement from Patrick Hawes' *Great War Symphony* which had its world premiere in the Royal Albert Hall on 9 October this year. This provides a very apt link back to the choir's 2014 commemorations. The singers, directed by David Ballard, will be joined by soloists Rosamund Walton (who coincidentally sang the words of Edith Cavell at the 2014 Sheringham Remembrance Concert) and Julian Chou-Lambert, together with an invited chamber orchestra.

The Menin Gate Memorial to the Missing at Ieper (Ypres)

MEMORIAL TO THE MISSING

In the biggest membership event in its history, The Royal British Legion recently recreated its 1928 pilgrimage to World War One battlefields.

A decade after the end of WW1, the British Legion (as it was then known) organised for veterans and war widows to visit the battlefields of the Somme and Ypres before marching to the Menin Gate at Ypres on 8th August 1928. This is the spot which hundreds of thousands of British and Commonwealth troops would have passed on the way to the battlefields of the Ypres Salient.

The Menin Gate Memorial to the Missing in what is now officially known as Ieper, Belgium, is dedicated to the British and Commonwealth soldiers who were killed in the Ypres Salient of World War One and whose graves are unknown. This memorial bears the names of more than 54,000 soldiers. Even today, every night at 8.00 pm a moving ceremony takes place under the Menin Gate. The Last Post Ceremony has become part of the daily life there and the local people

are proud of this simple but moving tribute to the courage and self-sacrifice of those who fell in defence of their town.

Exactly 90 years later, thousands of Legion representatives recreated the 1928 pilgrimage and visited the same battlefields. Then, on 8th August 2018, they paraded their branch standard and a wreath along the same route to the Menin Gate for the One Hundred Days ceremony to commemorate the last 100 days of WW1 and represent an entire generation that served while defending their country.

Sheringham and District Royal British Legion Branch Standard Bearer, Eddie Mayell and his wife Clare, attended the GP90 parade to represent the local community. Clare carried a wreath signed by The Mayor of Sheringham, Madeleine Ashcroft, as well as local youth groups and organisations. Prior to going out to Belgium, Eddie and Clare visited schools and other organisations, to give presentations with information about the event.

THE HOME FRONT IN SHERINGHAM

One hundred years ago Sheringham was a very different place to what it is today. None of us can help feeling the emotions of those days as now we commemorate some of the major events of the First World War.

The war years were an interesting time in the town, not only with our young men leaving their homes and venturing out into the outside world, but also these were times when more of that outside world came into Sheringham. There was concern that the quiet fishing village on the coast of the North Sea (German Ocean) and near to the deep waters of Weybourne could be a place for invasion. Soon peace was shattered by the sounds of marching feet, horses' hooves and the rumble of wheels or the wagons they pulled. The infantry and horse artillery had moved in.

The men were billeted in the town, staying at first in the hotels and then boarding houses and ordinary homes. For the duration of the war, furniture from the hotels was removed and stored in country houses around Norfolk. The troops and the locals took a while to adjust to each other, but after this initial period they very much became part of the community. Many ended up marrying local girls and took them back to their homes away from Sheringham. Some, after the war, brought their wives back to Sheringham to set up homes and businesses here.

The town was affected by war-time regulations on 'blackout' and air raids, with access to certain military installations being restricted. The most immediate impact. and certainly one that has lived long in the memory, was the dropping of a bomb from a Zeppelin, which was said to be the first to land on British soil. This incendiary bomb was dropped by Zeppelin on 19th January 1915

On the horizon the fleet passes Sheringham

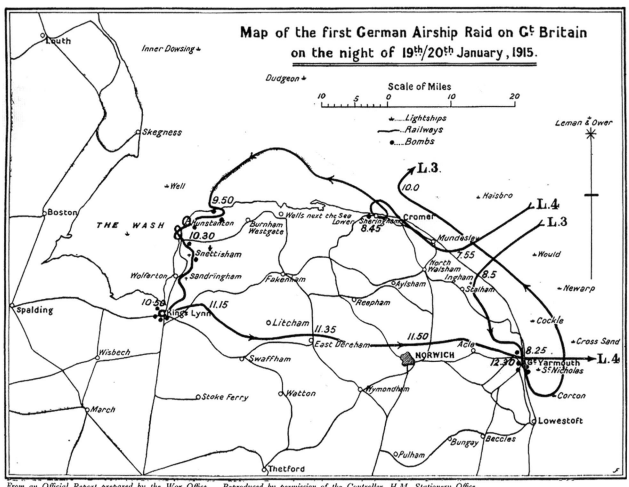

Map of the first German Airship Raid on Gᵗ Britain on the night of 19th/20th January, 1915.

Scale of Miles

..... Lightships
—— Railways
• .... Bombs

From an Official Report prepared by the War Office. Reproduced by permission of the Controller, H.M. Stationery Office.

and fell through the roof of a house at the end of Whitehall Yard. Luckily the bomb didn't explode and Bill Barney, a local fireman, removed it in a bucket. Mr A J Sadler of Church Street retained part of the casing and this is now on display in the First World War area in Sheringham Museum where you can read more about the incident.

Many of the troops who returned to Sheringham came back in times of peace and settled in the area they had been attracted to during the war years. Much has been recorded about these days in the former sleepy fishing village, some of which can be found in the books and displays in Sheringham Museum.

Needless to say, changes took place in the town, two of which became an important part of Sheringham for many years through the 20th century. It was in 1914 that Mr C A Sadler opened the Regent on Cromer Road to show silent films

Model of bomb dropped from Zeppelin on Sheringham during first raid on England on 19th January 1915

and, in 1916, the then Lord Mayor of London, Sir Charles Wakefield, opened the Sheringham Branch of the National Children's Home on Hook's Hill Road.

Tim Groves

SHERINGHAM

THE FIRST PLACE TO HAVE A ZEPELLIN BOMB DROPPED ON IT DURING THE FIRST WORLD WAR
Tuesday 19th January 1915 at 8.35 p.m.

THE ZEPPELIN RAID
A Report by our Special Correspondent

THE WEEKLY PRESS 23rd January 1915
THE AIR RAID
FOUR LIVES LOST AIRSHIPS SEEN BY MANY PEOPLE

Details of the air raid on the Norfolk coast gathered on Wednesday show that four persons were killed - two in Lynn and two in Yarmouth. It is difficult to ascertain how many bombs were dropped, but from accounts to hand it appears the numbers are as under:

Yarmouth 5 Sheringham 3 Lynn 7 Dersingham 1 Grimston 1 Heacham 1 Snettisham 1

There is no doubt that the raiders were Zeppelins, not aeroplanes, and probably three in number. At points in their voyage they showed searchlights and dropped flares and this enabled people to see them, though for the most part the voyage was made without any illuminant. One of the aircraft which passed over Runton was seen by almost the entire population of the parish.

A great deal of damage was done to property at Yarmouth and Lynn, especially at the latter place. The village of Snettisham also suffered considerably. The exploding bombs were heard at a great distance. The detonations at Yarmouth were heard at Lowestoft, and caused a good deal of excitement.

The story diligently circulated in certain quarters on Wednesday that one of the Zeppelins had been brought down at Hunstanton is untrue.

From Hunstanton comes a story which cannot be confirmed that the enemy were assisted in their flight along the coast by a motor car travelling in the same direction and carrying powerful lights.

The airships seen off the north coast of Holland steering west at about noon on Tuesday were reported from the same spots on their return journey in the small hours of Wednesday morning. The master of the St. Nicholas lightship off Yarmouth saw one of the Zeppelins arrive from the east about 8.30 p.m. and saw one returning from land just after midnight.

The German official report on the raid states that airships undertook an attack on "some fortified places on the English East Coast" and successfully dropped several bombs. The airships were shot at but returned unhurt.

(FROM A SPECIAL CORRESPONDENT - SHERINGHAM, Wednesday)

"This morning everything is calm and peaceful in this popular North Norfolk watering place. The Zeppelin visit on Tuesday evening is, of course, the one topic of the day, but the residents appear in no way excited or disturbed by the attention paid to the locality by the hostile aircraft. Nearly everyone seems to have heard or seen the mysterious visitors, and although accounts differ as to their number and the distance they ventured near the ground, it is the general opinion that the town escaped in a marvellous manner.

From what can be gathered, the fleet of aircraft approached the coast off Bacton, and whilst some turned to the south-east and went away towards Yarmouth, others steered due west towards Cromer and Sheringham and along the North Norfolk coast. At Cromer everything was in darkness, but residents could plainly hear the loud thumping of the engines of the aerial visitors. The noise, it was declared, was altogether different from that of an aeroplane engine, the throbbing of which has by this time become almost familiar to the Cromer people, who hardly pay any attention to the flight of a monoplane or a biplane. From Cromer to Sheringham it is only about four miles as the crow flies, and at 8.35 p.m. Mr. R.C. West, a coal merchant, who was on duty as a special constable, with Mr. Gooch at the Gas Works, near the Sheringham Hotel, saw a huge body floating in the air, and apparently coming from the direction of the lifeboat sheds. The night, although a little

hazy, was "decently fair" and there was no wind. The airship which had a tremendously long body, and looked like a gigantic sausage, travelled across the golf links, and was then lost sight of. A little later, perhaps half an hour afterwards, Mr. West and his fellow special saw another large airship - they are not sure whether it was not the first one circling back again - but for all that they plainly saw the

Zeppelin, although they could not estimate its distance from the ground. It came from almost the same direction as the aircraft they had previously seen, and after again hovering over the town went off northwards, that is over the sea. Mr. West says that on the first occasion he saw a light shown and also heard a bomb drop, whilst residents at the Sheringham Hotel state that the airship manoeuvered over the building, and turned a searchlight on.

From what we can learn two bombs were dropped in the town, and one just outside at Beeston. Two fell clear of all buildings, and beyond making holes in the ground did no damage; but from the third one the family of Mr. Robert Smith of Whitehall Gardens, Windham Road, a small street within 100 yards of the sea front, had a wonderful escape. Whitehall Gardens is a short cul de sac running southwards from Windham Road, and the Smith's cottage is a small dwelling at the top right hand corner. This morning it was the centre of a great deal of attraction, many of the residents and people from a distance visiting the little homestead and viewing the havoc which had been wrought upon the fabric and contents of the house. Mr. and Mrs. Smith were sitting in the kitchen with their little girl about half-past eight on Tuesday evening when the bomb came through their roof, passed through the bedroom and ceiling of the kitchen, and buried itself in the floor but a few inches from where the child was sitting. How the little girl escaped injury is most extraordinary. She was sitting close to the copper which adjoins the door from the kitchen to the sitting room, and is not more than a yard from the back door. The bomb fell on the tiles about a couple of feet from the eaves smashing its way through the roof and the ceiling. A bedstead in its path was shattered, the window glass broken by the concussion and the paper on the walls burnt and discoloured. The bedroom floor was burst through to about

the space of a square yard and the missile buried itself in the kitchen floor, but a few inches from the child's feet, and but a short distance from the front door. Fortunately the bomb did not explode. If it had, the house and probably those adjoining must have been wrecked. Mr. Smith, with great presence of mind, got his wife and the child out of the cottage, and then realised that an aerial attack was being made on the town, and he shook his fist at the aircraft as it disappeared. The force of the contact with the floor was so great as to break the chair on which the girl was sitting and to throw her to the floor. In a few minutes the police and soldiers arrived upon the scene and took possession of the bomb, which had not exploded, the fuse cap being found close to the door. The bomb which was about five inches across and six inches deep was sharply pointed at the lower end, and the upper end must have also been conical in shape. It was of a greyish green colour, with a red band round it.

The other bomb that fell on the town found a resting place on a piece of building ground belonging to Mr. W.M. Burton of Norwich and situated at the sea end of Priory Road."

"It was from Cromer, writes our correspondent, that Norwich was first advised of the presence of hostile aircraft on the Norfolk coast. About eight o'clock some Zeppelins approached the coast from the east, and then separated. Some took a south-westerly course, going in the direction of Yarmouth, and two more made for Cromer and Weybourne district. The noise made was nothing so much as

like the motors of half a dozen military cars doing the pace. The outline of at least one airship was seen as it passed over Cromer. The town was in practical darkness, for the absence of street and other lights has been a feature for some time.

Persons walking along the Runton Road saw distinctly what was not inaptly described as a glorified sausage gliding overhead. It was seen that at Runton the Zeppelin went seaward, coming in again to the westward of Sheringham where it encircled the church of Upper Sheringham and then making a circuit of the town and Beeston Hills went north-westerly over the water.

There seems to be some diversity of opinion as to whether there was one or more aerial visitors. The general trend seems to confirm first impressions that there were at least two, and that one was not a Zeppelin but an airship reconnoitering. Certainly at Runton the aircraft, which circled back from the Sheringham direction, seemed to hover as though uncertain which route to take. The Cromer Gas Works were not far away, and eventually after making circuits two or three times over Wyndham Park Cottages, East Runton, it steered north-westerly seaward. The noise of its return approach from the westward had been plainly heard at Cromer, where it seemed to be overhead. Whether Cromer was intended and Sheringham "landed" is open to question, but not a few think that they may have been the objective of the raiders."

Research and editorial by Tim Groves

STITCHES IN TIME

In 2016, as part of the important commemorations of the events and lives of people during the 1914–18 war, Sheringham Museum held a major exhibition after the opening of its new 'Top Deck': *"Stiches in Time: The knitting campaign of the First World War"*. This explained the forgotten battle fought on the Home Front to equip 'Tommy' with knits to help him survive.

Caught by surprise in a war that was supposed to last a few months, a whole host of items were knitted by women in Sheringham and throughout the country to plug the shortfall in the frontline supply chain essential to winning the war. From socks to slings, balaclavas to bandages, museum volunteers lovingly recreated items knitted during 1914–1918 from the original patterns and instructions issued to the public. Sheringham played a key part in the war effort with local knitting drives and events being organised.

When thinking started about how the Museum was going to commemorate WW1's 100th anniversary, a search through items that had been collected over the years brought to light those artefacts, photographs and information that we soon realised had an important story to tell about those who stayed at home whilst their men folk went to the Western Front.

The men had gone to France and were fighting in the trenches, where tens of thousands died, whilst on the Home Front, many women were doing their bit for the war effort by knitting, nursing and taking on other occupations like working in munitions factories.

"For the women, producing knitted clothing proved to be integral in winning the war. While the knitwear was primarily made to maintain and treat the health of the troops, it was also an expression of emotional support. The production of the knitwear was also beneficial to the knitters as it allowed them to constructively channel their own anxieties." (Introduction to Stitches in Times).

The knitting, that when completed only took a few days to reach the troops, built a strong bond between those fighting on the battlefields and the Home Front.

"The Home Front knitting campaign was driven by women who gathered in groups to knit, often in church halls, the vicarage and large houses. The groups offered an opportunity for the women to come together with a common goal, offered time to socialise and support each other. Often when the women knitted someone read aloud stories and newspaper articles or would sing knitting songs. Recordings of some of these feature in the exhibition. These groups helped to unite the community and foster a supportive environment to recover from the loss and trauma of war."

A TOWN AT WAR

Engineers at Marble Arch, Sheringham

Horse and gun carriage at Sheringham Park

Plane landed at Sheringham Park

Local lads at the bottom of Beeston Hill

War time beach precautions

Miss Upcher and convalescing officers

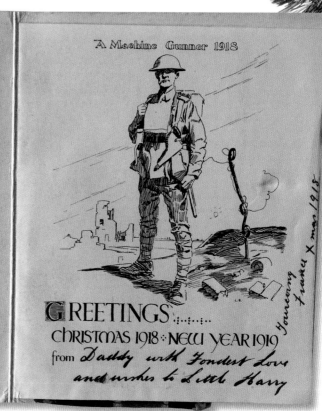

Buckingham Palace. O.H.M.S.

The General Officer Comdg. Machine
Gun Training Centre Grantham.

I have received your telegram
with much pleasure. Please
assure all ranks how proud I am
to be Colonel-in-Chief of the
Machine Gun Corps which has
gained so high a reputation for
efficiency and gallantry in the
field. I shall always follow their
doings with the keenest interest.

18.10.18   George R.I. Colonel-in-Chief.

A Machine Gunner 1918

GREETINGS ··········
CHRISTMAS 1918 ·· NEW YEAR 1919
from *Daddy with Fondest Love
and wishes to Little Harry*

Yourvery France X mas 1918

In Action

1918 Christmas greetings from Daddy with silk flag and pressed flower

© Tim Groves Archive

V.A.D. Auxiliary Hospital,
Sheringham in 1918

MEDICAL/HOSPITAL WORKERS

Dr Linnell and his wife (who was Commandant of the Hospital) are in the centre of the photograph above, taken outside the hospital.

The medical workers listed here worked at the Auxiliary Red Cross Hospital at the top of Vincent Road/Cliff Road in Sheringham or The Dales Red Cross Hospital in Upper Sheringham (now a hotel). Many were born in the town, whilst others came from around the country to work here. Some of the others named were Sheringham born, but worked in hospitals outside the area (eg London and Cromer), including the front line overseas.

The conscientious objectors, the Ardley brothers, are included. They worked for the Red Cross Field Ambulance Unit in France. See page 32 for more details of them.

Also listed below are those who worked in a domestic capacity (as stated where possible). Marital status is indicated where known.

This list is by no means exhaustive and is taken from various sources. The nurses were volunteer nurses. It is not possible to list all regular, qualified nurses as they are not all detailed on the Red Cross site. Some sources are of the time so there may be errors and omissions. Sheringham Museum would be interested in any information (particularly photographs, letters, etc) with regard to those listed, or those who have been omitted.

ALDIS, Miss Anne

ALPE, Mrs Isabel Ruth

ARDLEY, Mr Alan Frederick

ARDLEY, Mr Basil

ARDLEY, Mr Francis

ARKWRIGHT, Miss Olive Katherine Mary

ASHFORD, Miss Mary Crisp (maid/cook)

BORDER, Miss Olive May (waitress)

(BURTON) COOK, Miss Clara Francis

CARTER, Miss Rosa Elizabeth

CHADWYCK-HEALEY (née Charrington), Mrs Gwendolen Mary

CLARKE, Miss Mabel

COUTTS, Mrs Eleanor

CRASKE, Miss Mabel Sarah (housework)

CREMER, Miss Ida

CUNNINGHAM, Miss Edith

EDWARDS, Mr John

FISHER, Miss Bertha (housemaid duties)

FROST, Miss Edith Mary (assistant cook)

GREEN, Mrs Jessie (cook VAD Hospital)

GURNEY, Miss Anne (homeworker)

HAVARD, Miss Emma

HOCH, Miss Valerie

HOWARD, Miss Emma

JACKSON, Mrs Blanche Marion

KING, Mrs Margaret (Commandant The Dales)

LAMBERT, Miss Sarah

LEE, Miss Nora (cook)

LINNELL, Mrs Agnes (Commandant VAD Hospital)

LINNELL, Dr James Everard (Medical Doctor)

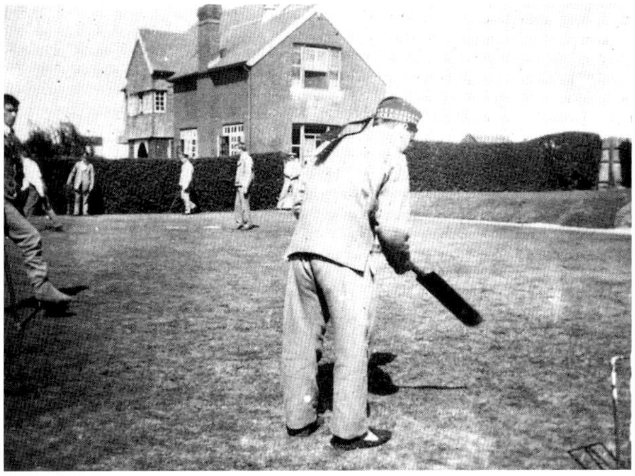

A spot of cricket for convalescing soldiers

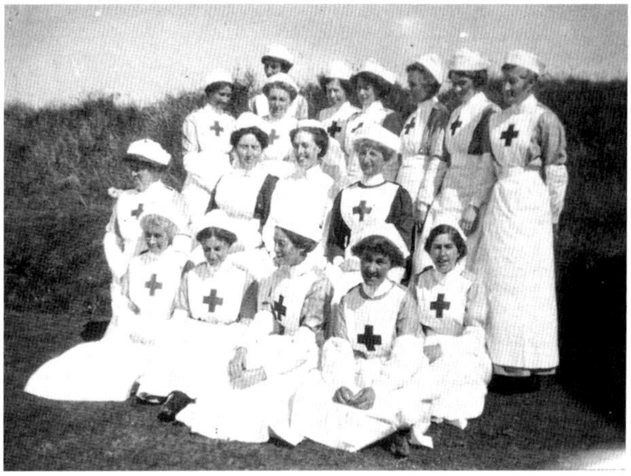

Red Cross nurses

LITTLE (Mrs Stimson), Miss Margaret
LOVETT, Miss Doris
MARRIOTT, Miss Dorothea
MARRIOTT, Miss Gertrude Dorothea
MCFARLANE, Miss Catherine
MINNS, Miss Enid May
OLLEY, Miss Mabel Elizabeth
O'FFLAHERTIE, Miss Grace (Matron, VAD Hospital)
PALMER, Mrs May Lilian
PEMBERTON, Mrs Eva
PERCIVAL, Miss Marion
PYGOTT, Miss Nora
SLAUGHTER, Miss Julia Ann Louise (Nursing probationer)
TURNER, Mrs Jill Helen
UPCHER, Miss Christine Mary
UPCHER, Miss Edith
UPCHER, Miss Laura ('odd jobs')
WAKEFIELD, Miss Elsie Frances (masseuse)
WATERS, Mrs Alice
WATSON, Miss Dorothy (housework)
WESTON, Miss Annie Elizabeth (housework)
WESTON, Miss Maud Elsie (housework)
WHARTON, Miss May
WILLIAMS, Miss Gladys (occasional nurse)
WOOD-SMITH, Mrs Evelyn

Compiled by Jane Crossen, with reference to previous research by Lesley Lougher and Jan Hillier

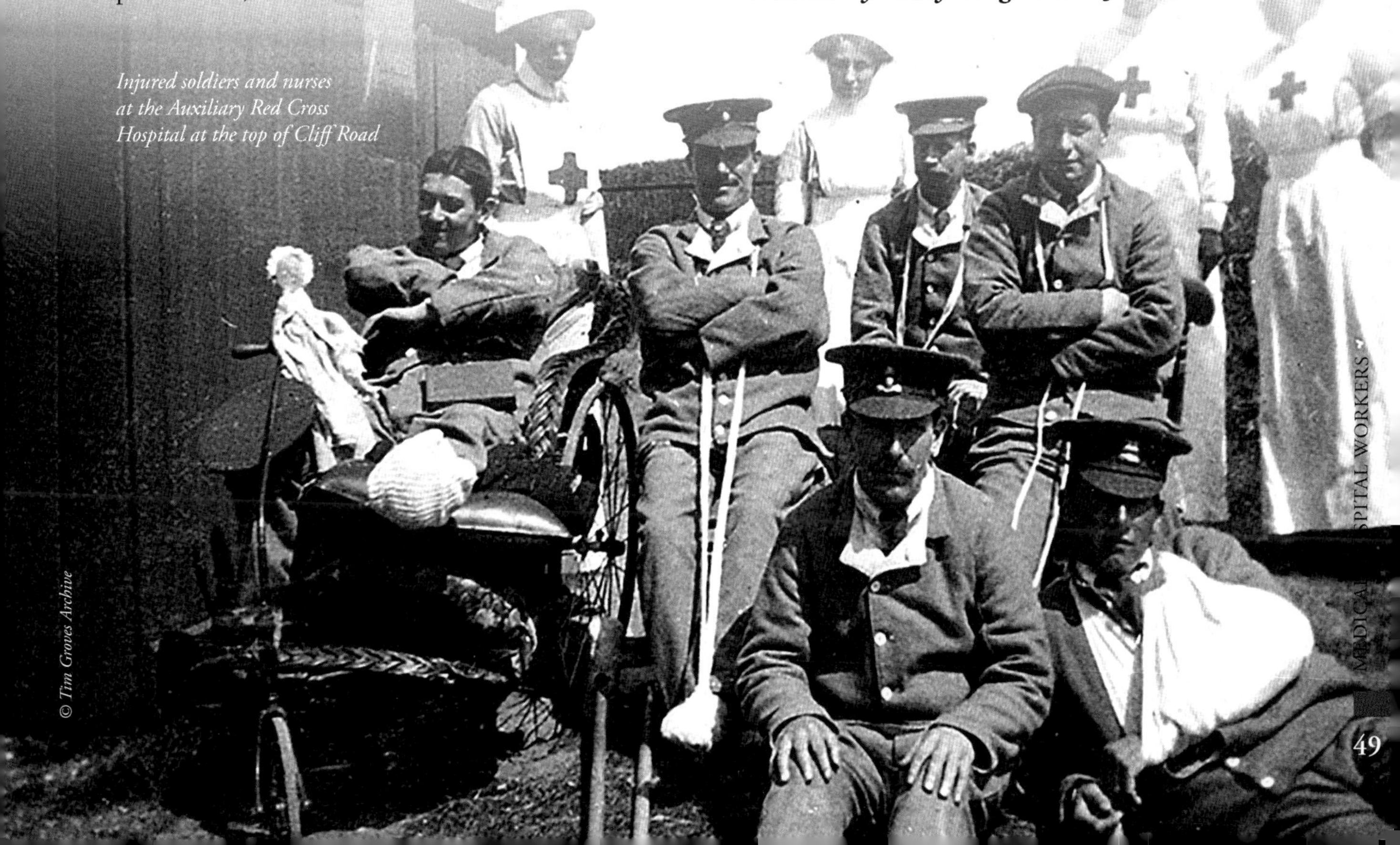

Injured soldiers and nurses at the Auxiliary Red Cross Hospital at the top of Cliff Road

LILIAN LUBBOCK'S AUTOGRAPH BOOK

Lilian Maud Lubbock was born in Sheringham in November 1900 to Samuel and Joanna Lubbock (nee Steward). Samuel was a house painter and decorator and so will have been a well-known face around town.

In 1914 she wrote her name and year in a new autograph book. She was 14.

During the coming war years a fascinating selection of ditties, poems, verses and signatures were written in the book from serving soldiers, friends and family. Some of them that appear to be original poems written in the book are particularly interesting. Here is one written by a serving soldier:

For you sweet maid these lines I write
My thoughts are all of you tonight
When far away you still are near
In my dreams a fair vision you appear

How clothed with beauty are the woods in Spring
With sunshine and flowers, we feel we must sing
But far lovelier yet, your sweet face I see
Bringing sunshine and gladness all day to me

To be with you always, and hear your sweet voice
To love and to care for you, that is my choice
If kind fate wills that this should be so
Dear heart what happiness we two would know

Nov 1917

Lilian's autograph book

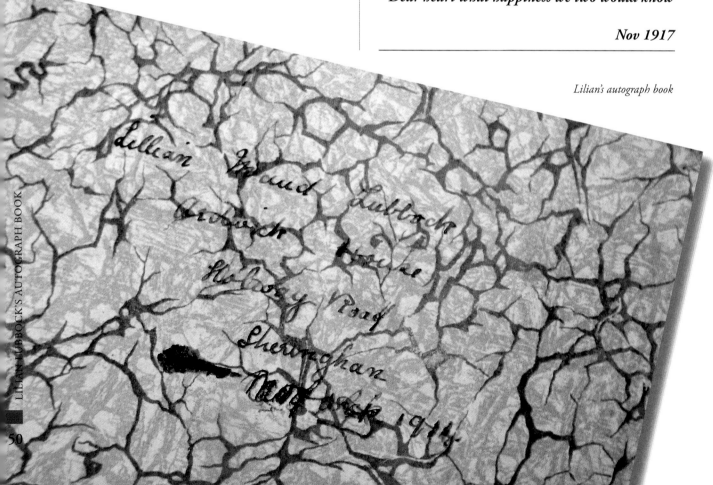

To be with you always, and hear your sweet Voice
To love and to care for you, that is my choice,
If kind fate wills that this should be so,
Dear heart what happiness we two would know.

The previous November he had written some lines taken from a very long poem by Byron. He entitled it *'Love'* but the actual poem it is taken from is *'The Giaour: A Fragment of a Turkish Tale'*. Interestingly, he has changed the word 'Allah' to 'God' in his version:

Love

Yes! Love, indeed, is light from Heaven,
A spark of that immortal fire –
With angels shared – by God given
To lift from Earth our low desire
Devotion wafts the mind above
But Heaven itself descends in Love:
A feeling from thee Godhead caught
To learn from self each sordid thought;
A ray of Him who formed the whole
A glory circling round the Soul

(Byron)

(Transcribed into Lilian's autograph book 24th November 1916.)

Just two poems written by a lonely soldier far from home? Research has uncovered that the soldier who wrote those lines was Reuben Samuel Tebbott, a lance-corporal in the 14th Suffolks. At the beginning of the war he was 25.

Lilian's birth was registered in the last quarter of 1900, so it is thought that he is penning poems on her birthday That means she's just 16 when he wrote the Byron poem in her book.

They married in 1920 – Lilian is 20, Samuel is 31.

Reading the autograph book, and knowing what happened after the war, is quite interesting. Various people seem to allude to the relationship, although it is unclear whether her mother knew!

They returned to London (Samuel's birthplace) and had only one child. Samuel died in London in 1953. From a Jewish family, he had worked in tailoring all his life. Lilian returned to the same address she wrote in the front of her autograph book way back in 1914. This we know as her probate states she died there in 1980, aged 80.

Margery, her sister, does not appear to marry or move out from Ardwick House, let alone Sheringham. She is on the 1939 register with her parents there and she died in Sheringham in 1993 aged 90. Someone in Sheringham must know of her?

Interestingly, whilst researching Olive Edis' godson's family tree (he is a Woodhouse and lived in Sheringham) it was discovered that he and Lilian are related. David's father Valentine (a conscientious objector in WW2 who died tragically in 1945 in Oxford) was a cousin of Lilian's.

Here are some family references from the autograph book. It would appear her cousin may well have had an inkling of the blossoming love...

"Never trouble trouble
Till trouble troubles you
You'll only double trouble
And trouble others too"

With Love Margery
April 1 1916

Be a good girl
Lead a good life
Find a good husband
Make a good wife

Cousin Sallie (or Lallie)

Dec 25th 1916

Here's Jolly Good Luck
To the girl that loves a soldier I "hear hear"

Love from Sallie (or Lallie?)

25 Oct (probably 1916)
Melton Constable

God holds the key of all unknown
And I am glad
If other hand should hold the key
Or if he trusted it to me
I might be sad.

(with love mother)

Here are two of the wonderful poems from the autograph book: unread for nearly 100 years:

A Soldier's Wife

Oh, I'm tired of the home – there is so much to do
It is a marvel to me how I ever get through

From the moment I'm up till it's bed time again
I keep at it hard just a long weary train

Dull trying jobs and each day they get more
Oh who'd be a housewife in these days of War

And then there's the chicks they are dear things of course
But really I need to be as strong as a horse

With their washing and mending and meals to get done
And of course they are noisy and full of their fun

I love them, but sometimes they wear me quite out
Oh a wife and mother works hard there's no doubt.

And it's lonely this evening now Jack is away
Although I'd be the last one to bid him to stay

My brave soldier husband it makes my heart ache
To think of him out there the risks he must take

And the hardships and dangers oh what must they be
Yet my man writes such brave cheery letters to me

Yes, brave cheery letters in spite of it all
Though he fights and he suffers and brave comrades fall

And here I am grousing and fretting each day
Because of my hardships while he is away

To the cause, to his regiment, he's loyal and game
Enduring and cheerful and I'll be the same

For we women can help do our share in the War

The home is my Regiment
My duty lies there

A Woman's Bit

(Sadly, unsigned, unnamed and undated but entries in the book either side are dated the end of April and early May 1916 and it is almost certainly written by a Sheringham woman)

Four Crosses

First – emblem of a soul's desire
The craved for hardly won VC
Gained by fierce bangs through blood and fire
The brave deed done on land and sea

'Legion of Honours' - the second cross
So proudly borne upon the breast
By martial Frenchmen scorning loss
Of life or limb who gave their best

'The Military Cross' – the third
A grand reward for him who bears
That sign that shows his King has heard
Honours his bravery – and cares

Ah! Little cross rough cross of wood
That crowns a heroes rest in state
Fourth cross which stiffly upright stood
Marks just a simple soldier's fate

Winifred Gran. brell?? (Name indecipherable)
Undated

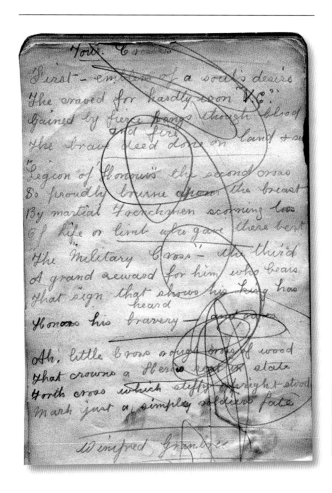

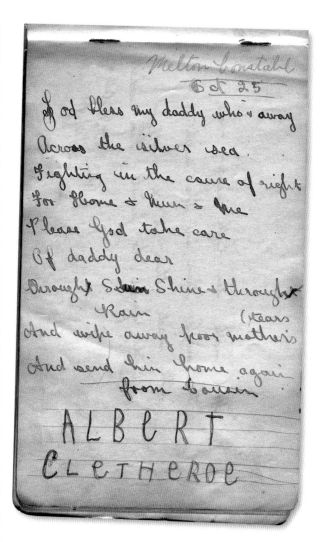

And finally, this sad little verse written by a little boy to his daddy far away...he is Albert Cletheroe and his handwriting makes him about 5 or 6. He appears to be Lilian's cousin living in Melton Constable.

God bless my daddy who is away
Across the silver sea
Fighting in the cause of right
For home and mum and me

Please God take care
Of daddy dear
Through shine and through rain
And wipe away poor mother's tears
And send him home again.

Researched and compiled by Jane Crossen

Extracts published with permission of Sheringham Museum

THE MERCANTILE MARINES

At Tower Hill in London, there is a monument listing the names of the 11,900 fishermen and merchant seafarers who lost their lives during WW1 and have no known grave but the sea (pictured below). They were known as the Mercantile Marines – later to become the Merchant Navy.

Those who died did not all receive medals but their regiment is referred to as Mercantile Marine and they are listed on the Tower Hill memorial and described as being granted a 'Debt of Honour'.

By the end of the war, nearly 1,500 trawlers and 1,400 steam drifters had been requisitioned for various tasks, particularly minesweeping and anti-submarine work. Fishing during the First World War was an extremely hazardous business. In all, some 394 British fishing boats on war service and 675 non-combatant fishing boats were sunk. A total of 434 fishermen lost their lives.

There is some controversy around the fact that the memorial has never been featured on the BBC's coverage of Remembrance Sunday.

One of those vessels was the *Frigate Bird*, which was captured and sunk off Flamborough Head on 28 June 1917. Its exact fate is unknown as she went out alone but some reports have it that she was torpedoed by the German submarine *UC 63*.

The crew of five were lost and their bodies never recovered. They included three men who were born in Sheringham and the son of one of the men: he was just 16 years old. Christopher and William Sadler were brothers.

FARROW, John William (38), deckhand. Born in Sheringham (husband of Fearlene Farrow (née Love)). Lived at 94, Ladysmith Road, Grimsby.

SADLER, Christopher (49), skipper. Born in Sheringham (husband of Maria Sadler (née Green)). Lived at 162, Victor Street, Grimsby.

SADLER, Horice Samuel (16), deckhand. Born in Grimsby (son of Maria Sadler (née Green)). Lived at 162, Victor Street, Grimsby.

SADLER, William Richard (60), deckhand. Born in Sheringham (Husband of Ann Sophia Sadler). Lived at 32, Fraser Street, Grimsby.

Ten Sheringham men are listed as having been awarded service medals in the Mercantile Marines:

BROWN, Sydney	born 1888
CRASKE, Abraham	born 1888
FARROW, Robert	born 1866
GRICE, Robert Henry	born 1876
MIDDLETON, Bennett Greet	born 1888
PRICE, William Thomas	born 1896
SADLER, William Richard	born 1857
SADLER, Christopher Joel	born 1867
WEST, James Henry	born 1879
WEST, George Enos	born 1880

Researched and compiled by Jane Crossen

READY TO FACE THE ELEMENTS OR THE ENEMY
THE BRAVERY OF THE SHERINGHAM LIFEBOATMEN

During the war years, the work of Sheringham's lifeboats the *J.C. Madge* and the *Henry Ramey Upcher* went on. Often during wartime rescue attempts the two lifeboats worked together.

The *J.C. Madge* was called out on 16th November 1914, to return three R.N.V.R. officers to their boat off Cley. On her return to Sheringham she was called to the assistance of the *S.S. Vera*, off Cley Beach. Getting no reply to her signals, the *J.C. Madge* returned to her station in what was a strong easterly gale. The next day, the Cley lifesaving team and local fishermen took off the crew of the *Vera*. The rescued men said they had seen the signals but did not reply as they thought the conditions were so bad. They had feared the lifeboat would have been wrecked if she had attempted a rescue.

In February 1916, the lifeboat was called out in gale conditions, in what could only be described as a blinding snow-storm. A steamship, *S.S. Uller*, out of Bergen, was in difficulties. Coxswain Obadiah Cooper gave the men a choice as to whether they should set off, because the weather was so bad.

Launch of the J.C. Madge

With some difficulty they managed to launch and found the *Uller* off Blakeney. The *J.C. Madge* accompanied the ship while she made for Grimsby, finally arriving in the Humber 48 hours later. The crew were exhausted. One crew member, Jimmy 'Paris' West, recalled that their frozen clothing had to be cut off with a knife. Coxswain Obadiah Cooper had to have special treatment for his eyes, which had been damaged by flying spray as he stood exposed steering the lifeboat.

In April 1918, the *J.C. Madge* went to the rescue of the *Alice Taylor*, a collier from Dundee. The crew ended up standing by while another vessel began to tow her to Yarmouth. Off Sea Palling, the *Alice Taylor* started to sink and the crew of 18 had to leap into the lifeboat. One man fell into the sea and risked being crushed by the lifeboat and ship rolling together. Fortunately, he was plucked to safety.

Clearly it was not just those Sheringham men who went off to war who faced extreme dangers – the lifeboat crews risked their lives every time they were launched, in war or peace.

Tim Groves

DORIS HEWITT'S SCRAPBOOKS

Doris Hewitt was born in Ealing, London in 1888 into a very wealthy family. They had many servants and were living in Kensington at the beginning of World War One.

They also had a home in Sheringham: 'Eastcourt', at the bottom of Holt Road. Today it is private flats. Way back then it would have been a formidable house overlooking the town towards the sea.

Doris spent a lot of time there with her parents, Thomas and Theodora, and her brothers George Graily (often referred to as Graily) and Cecil. Cecil, who had a movement-limiting permanent disability, was given a camera and took hundreds of photographs, some of which are on display in Sheringham Museum. There are many of Doris, the family and their friends: before, during and just after WW1.

Doris started a scrapbook at the beginning of the war, which is annotated at the front, indicating that she would update it for the duration. Little did she know it would take five huge volumes to complete her task.

Her brother Graily served in the army but was never overseas. There are many references to soldiers in the books: perhaps friends or relatives. There are also a lot of reports of weddings and engagements!

Doris herself married Charles Pearse fairly late in life in 1929 at the age of 40, and continued to live in Sheringham (South Street) for some years. She died in 1949 at the age of 60 in Totnes, Devon, where she lived with her husband who died the year before her at the age of 83. She had no children.

The scrapbooks are housed at Sheringham Museum and are in the process of being digitised and researched. They are a rich resource: detailing national and local press cuttings, cartoons, names of Sheringham soldiers serving at the front, deaths, marriages, important fund-raising events in Sheringham and London and much more.

There were hundreds of flag days to raise money for the war effort across Great Britain and Doris seems to have bought a lot of them – they are stuck painstakingly into her scrapbooks.

Many thousands of volunteers contributed to the war effort by selling and producing what were known as 'flag day badges' and they generated a massive amount of money for all sorts of causes. It has been estimated that during World War One the Red Cross alone raised £22 million, the equivalent to £1.75 billion today!

The flags in Doris' scrapbook range from the 'Waifs and Strays Society' to the 'British Farmers' Red Cross Fund' and 'Help Ealing Soldiers & Sailors (broken in our wars)' and the rather reassuring 'Efficiency is Strength WVR (Women's Volunteer Reserve)'.

Opposite is a photograph of a page of flags neatly pinned into her scrapbook. She was the consummate perfectionist in keeping her scrapbooks – luckily for her future readers.

One of the pages headed 'Sheringham Emergency Committee' (dated Feb 1915 in pencil by Doris) is a fascinating read. Headings are: Aerial Bombardment, Naval Bombardment and even... the ultimate: INVASION!

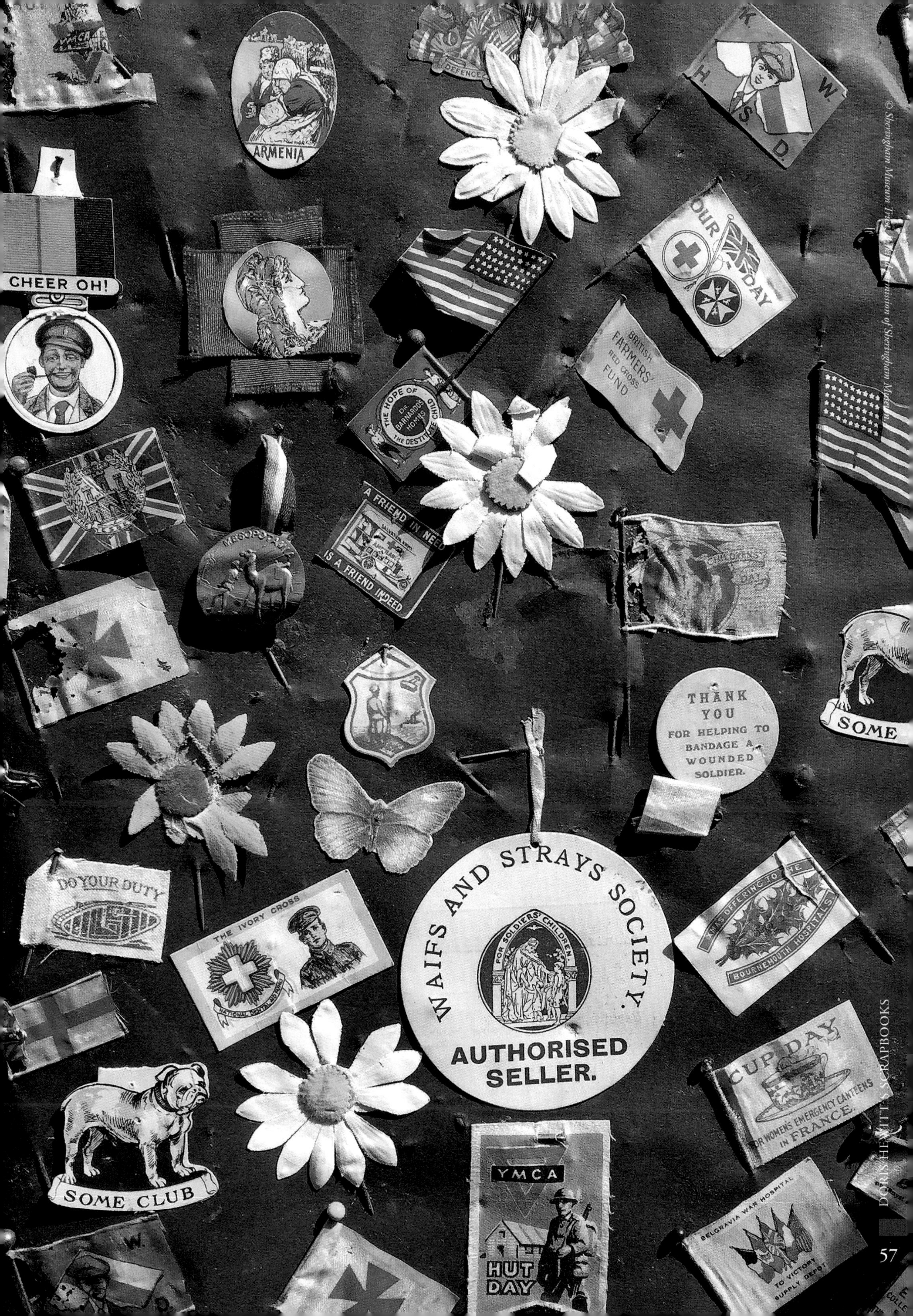
ARMENIA
CHEER OH!
K. H. W. S. D.
OUR DAY
BRITISH FARMERS' RED CROSS FUND
THE HOPE OF THE DESTITUTE CHILD
DR. BARNARDO'S HOMES
A FRIEND IN NEED IS A FRIEND INDEED
MESOPOTAMIA
CHILDREN'S DAY
THANK YOU FOR HELPING TO BANDAGE A WOUNDED SOLDIER.
SOME
DO YOUR DUTY
THE IVORY CROSS
NATIONAL DENTAL AID FUND
WAIFS AND STRAYS SOCIETY.
FOR SOLDIERS' CHILDREN.
AUTHORISED SELLER.
XMAS OFFERING TO THE BOURNEMOUTH HOSPITALS
CUP DAY
FOR WOMEN'S EMERGENCY CANTEENS IN FRANCE.
SOME CLUB
YMCA
HUT DAY
BELGRAVIA WAR HOSPITAL
TO VICTORY SUPPLY DEPOT

SHERINGHAM EMERGENCY COMMITTEE.

© Sheringham Museum Trust. By kind permission of Sheringham Museum.

Feb. 1915

It is most unlikely that we shall be subjected to bombardment from the sea, or that the enemy would be able to effect a landing, but the Committee has taken the precaution of arranging a plan of procedure to meet any contingency. The following directions are intended to be a guide for the public:—

AERIAL BOMBARDMENT.

Upon the approach of hostile aircraft all gas lights should be immediately turned out. The public should provide themselves with candles for use where it is imperative that some light should be used; they are warned against standing in the streets. The safest place is probably in the lower floor of their houses, in cellars, or dug-outs. If the Committee are able to obtain sufficient notice, St. Peter's Church Bells will be clashed as a warning to the public and a signal to Special Constables to proceed to their appointed stations.

The public on the whole have done their best to carry out the order with regard to lights but from a high point outside the town one evening recently there were about a dozen lights quite distinct. Upon investigation these lights in most cases were showing through divisions, or at the side, or bottom of curtains. It is not sufficient to drop a blind, a dark curtain must be used, and every occupier should take the precaution of examining his windows from the outside. It is most important for the safety of the town that no light whatever should be visible. Under the Defence of the Realm Act and the Orders made under the same it is a serious offence to fail to effectively obscure all public and private lights between the hours of 5 p.m. and 7-30 a.m.

NAVAL BOMBARDMENT.

In the event of bombardment from the sea, keep out of the streets as much as possible. Again, the safest place is probably in the house on the lower floor, in the room furthest from the sea, or in the cellar or dug-out. For those who prefer to leave their houses, the best places are on the land side of the railway banks, the south side of the Golf Links Hills and Beeston Hills, and in holes or pits such as those on the Golf Links, near Sweetbriar Lane, and the old Lime Kiln near Beeston Hills.

INVASION.

In the case of a hostile landing away from our own neighbourhood, the Military Authorities will decide whether it is necessary for the public to leave this district; in the case of a landing near us the decision will rest with the Committee, and in either case the necessary instructions will be conveyed to the public by the Police.

Should it be decided that the inhabitants must leave the town, those who can walk should proceed by one of the following routes:—

1.—The path through the Waterworks Wood.
2.—The road across Beeston Common past the Gamekeeper's Cottage.
3.—Brittain's Lane.
4.—The road through Mrs. Cremer's Yard at Beeston.

Out of Upper Sheringham the best road is past Heath Farm and across the Heath to the Mill.

The route will then be by East Beckham, Gresham, Itteringham Bridge, Saxthorpe, to Swaffham.

The public should take money, a few warm clothes, and as much food as convenient.

In case of meeting the Military, the public must leave the road and pass along in the fields until the Military have passed.

Those who are sick and infirm must proceed to the field on the Cromer Road between the Roman Catholic Church and the Railway Line, where transport will be provided.

The public must find food and shelter for themselves along the road when they wish to rest. Special Constables have instructions to help as much as possible.

Having arrived at Swaffham, the public must find shelter and food themselves. The Committee are arranging headquarters there at the Police Station, and they will do their best to help those who cannot provide for themselves.

The Committee will advise the public when it is safe to return, and, if possible, will arrange for their transport by rail or otherwise. It will, therefore, be advisable for everybody to report their temporary address at the Committee's Headquarters.

Civilians are particularly warned that they must on no account carry firearms or other weapons. These should be handed to the Police.

When closing your house always remember to turn off the gas at the meter.

All those inhabitants of Sheringham owning motor-cars, horses and conveyances of every description, bicycles, and any other form of transport, must on the alarm being given, either bring or send such transport to the field in the Cromer Road opposite the Roman Catholic Church. This is most important, as upon it will depend the safety of those who cannot walk, and of women and children.

The Committee desire to point out that owners of horses, carts, motors, etc., will not be allowed to use the roads at will, but that such transport must be vouched for by the Emergency Committee.

Rounce & Wortley, "Reliance" Works, Holt.

It is reproduced on the left from the page in her scrapbook:

"When closing your house always remember to turn off the gas at the meter." With enemy boots coming up the garden path, it is probably unlikely that would be the first thing on the minds of the locals heading for the path through Waterworks Wood or through Mrs Cremer's Yard at Beeston!

Below is another page of press cuttings with references to Sheringham. Some well-known local names there, not least Olive Edis, the famous war photographer, who lived in South Street, Sheringham and married into the Galsworthy family. She is buried in Sheringham cemetery.

There is a particularly interesting snippet in the scrapbook about a War Loan collection in Sheringham. Transcribed from a press cutting from un unknown publication and dated February 1917 (as written in pencil on the press cutting in Doris Hewitt's handwriting):

WAR LOAN IN
SHERINGHAM AND DISTRICT
OVER £25,000

The amount has exceeded all expectations. The official figures which reached us late last night are as follows: Through the Banks £20,500, and Post Office 4,800, making a total of: £25,300 in all. At the Post Office many hundreds of pounds in gold were paid in, in varying amounts, showing that even the poorest investor was proud to do his or her little bit. The total is regarded as extremely satisfactory.

Using values taken from various online historic money calculator websites and discarding the highest and lowest values and taking an average of the other amounts, it is the equivalent in today's money to around a staggering £1,443,845.25!

From a town with such a small population at that time, it is an astonishing amount of money: *'extremely satisfactory'* seems rather an understatement.

Researched and compiled by Jane Crossen

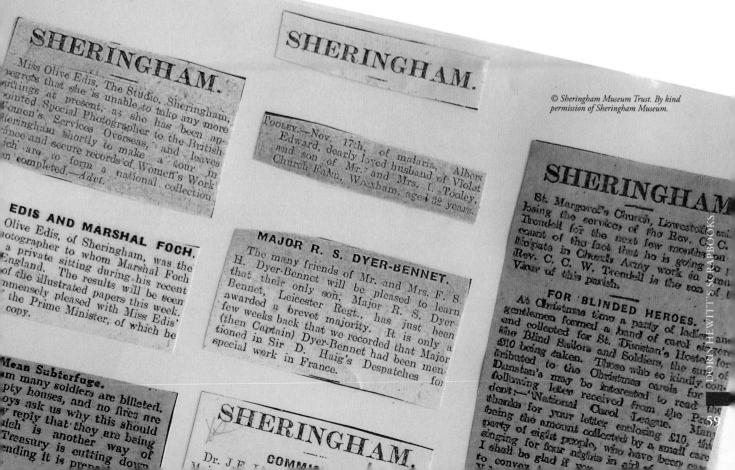

MY WORLD WAR ONE 'EXPERIENCES'

A mere 75 years old, how can I claim to have experienced World War One? I believe I can and that my experiences indicate that all of us are far more affected by the conflict than we realise.

My first 'experience' of World War One was about 70 years ago, with '*The Story of 25 Eventful Years in Pictures*', a book published to celebrate the Silver Jubilee of King George V. I read it, or rather looked at the pictures, many times as a young child and was always fascinated by the pictorial history of what were indeed 'eventful years'. Strange how the last 70 years have never seemed 'eventful' in the same way, even though in reality they have been much more so.

I can still recall the photo of Winston Churchill, the then Home Secretary, watching the siege of Sidney Street in 1911. (If you want a video treat of an old Pathe Newsreel, visit **https://goo.gl/**

bvVwTM) However, it was the photos of the Great War that fascinated me most.

Such was my level of interest and knowledge of the conflict until 2007. Whilst on holiday in France that year, we came across the Canadian National Vimy Memorial at Vimy Ridge and the nearby Vimy Memorial Park. Two facts brought home to me, very vividly, how horrifying the war was. Firstly, the memorial honours the 60,000 Canadians killed during the war, 3,598 of whom died at the Battle of Vimy Ridge. The names of 11,168 missing Canadians killed in action in France, whose remains have not been found or identified, are also listed on the memorial.

Secondly, a few hundred yards behind the memorial is Vimy Memorial Park. Here is a short section of trenches, which formed the Allied Front Line and the German Front line. These trenches would have muddy and rat-infested during the war, but today the duckboards and sandbags have been reinforced with concrete, to preserve them for tourists.

What really impacted me was just how close the Front lines were to each other. I had always thought of them as being at least half a mile apart. The reality is, there was sometimes only a few metres of No-Mans-Land between them.

The event that really showed me how affected I was by World War One was even more unexpected. In early 2009, I learned that my grandfather was killed on 23rd May 1918, when a bomb dropped on the hospital where he was working at St Omer in Northern France. I also discovered that he was buried at the Commonwealth Graves Cemetery at nearby Longuenesse (pictured left). He was 38 years old and my father would have been four

© Peter Farley

Reconstructed trenches at Vimy Ridge Memorial Park

years old just under four months later. So, he never knew his father.

We were going on holiday to France that spring, so I decided I would visit my grandfather's grave. Nothing could have prepared me for the emotional impact of that event. I can remember crouching down by the grave and 'introducing myself' to my long-dead grandpa. It was an incredibly cathartic experience, bringing closure that I had not realised needed to be brought.

The fact that I experienced such grief, although two generations separated us, caused me to consider the ripple effect of a single death in war. My sorrow, nearly one hundred years later, was very real. How much more the sorrow of those close to him, those who knew him and loved him. Perhaps a few dozen or so people were immediately affected by his death. Multiply that by two generations and again by 20 million (the number who died during WW1) and you gain some understanding of the combined grief this conflict caused.

Such experiences have caused me to realise how important it is to remember and honour those who gave their lives, albeit a hundred years ago.

Their sacrifices also motivated me to get involved in the Sheringham World War One Centenary Commemoration and Remembrance Project. Perhaps others will come to realise how affected they might be after reading this book?

Peter Farley

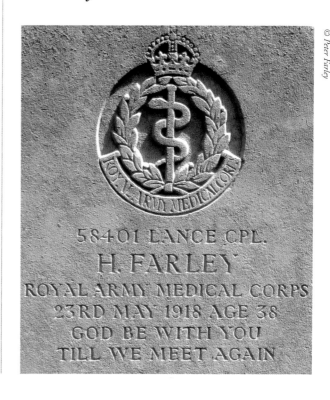

WINNER
Alexandra – Stretton Sugwas CE Academy

Children's artwork entries on the theme of war and remembrance

SHERINGHAM WI'S POPPIES

Sheringham WI thought long and hard about ways in which we could commemorate the end of World War One. We were keen to ensure that the whole community was reminded of the debt owed to those men and boys of Sheringham who left to fight for freedom, some of whom would never return.

One can picture the euphoric scene, as sons, fathers, brothers and friends cheerily left the town, amongst waving flags and perhaps, on some occasions, the local brass band. There would have been an air of excitement; after all it was going to be a great adventure. The Hun would be taught a lesson and they would be 'home for Christmas'. Among those sending the 'boys' off would have been the mums, grandmas and sisters of the WI.

It was very fitting, therefore, that Sheringham WI were, from the beginning, partners in the Sheringham World War One Centenary Commemoration and Remembrance Project in November 2018. It was felt that however the occasion was marked by the WI, it should in some way reflect the community's fishing heritage.

The WI decided to produce a poppy installation. The idea was to invite anyone, adults and children, to a free afternoon session crocheting, knitting or sewing poppies, with tea and biscuits (perhaps even cake!) providing the bait. In addition, the invitation went out to individuals, groups or organisations who wished to make, sew, knit, or crochet any poppies, which could also be used for this creation. The idea was to get as many people as possible involved.

One can imagine, as the hostilities began a hundred years ago, that the community would have wanted to play their part then too. In particular, the women would have been keen to join the war effort, knowing their country needed them to take up their needles.

I'm reminded of the *Stitches in Time* event, put on in 2016 by Sheringham Museum. This highlighted the knitting campaign of World War One, where folk were able to learn about local knitting drives and the work of the Queen Mary's Needle Work Guild in providing knitted bandages and essential clothing for the war effort. All this activity encouraged the public to produce items to help 'Tommy' keep warm in the trenches.

Now Sheringham WI can ensure that the endeavours of those who stayed behind will not be forgotten.

Liz Withington

WILL WE REMEMBER THEM?

A week or so after Upper Sheringham Parish Council had agreed to find ways of commemorating the end of World War One, John Dorey (the Parish Council Chair) stumbled across one very apt way of doing so. For some time, he had been thinking he should finish off a task his father had begun, before he passed away. The task he had decided on many years ago, but never finished, was to build some sort of wooden outbuilding.

His father had started to collect together the various pieces of wood etc, which he needed to build the structure. In the end, he got no further than leaning what he had gathered in a corner of his workshop. Here they had lain, just gathering dust, until John started to make preparations for what would effectively be a memorial to his father. As he started to move things, he came across a large piece of wood, which clearly was no ordinary piece of scrap material.

There, sandwiched between two boards, John discovered the plaque on the right. It was in such a good state, that it was tempting to think that his father had intended to preserve it. John believes his father probably came into possession of the plaque, when (many years ago) either the chapel or the village school were refurbished. John carried out some minor restoration and cleaned the plaque up, ready for it to be rededicated at a special service in Upper Sheringham Parish Church (All Saints), on Sunday

11th November 2018. This ceremony will be at the centre of the village commemorations.

This happenstance raises the question of how we preserve our memorials. The government publication – '*War Memorials in England and Wales: Guidance for Custodians*' – outlines the importance of preserving our war memorials. But what do we want to preserve? Is it the actual edifice, tablet or plaque? Architecturely speaking, it is. But isn't it what the memorial stands for that we wish to preserve – in this case the sacrifice made by so many? I believe legislation gives us an opportunity to creatively consider this important issue. Section 1 of *War Memorials (Local Authorities' Powers) Act 1923* empowers local authorities to incur reasonable expenditure for the maintenance, repair and protection of war memorials within their control. That is the letter of the Law but what is the Spirit of the Law?

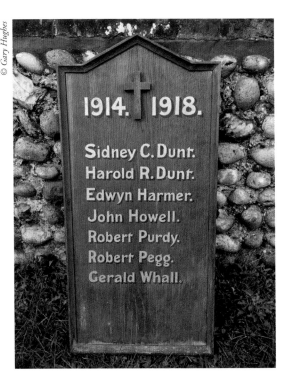

© Gary Hughes

1914. 1918.

Sidney C. Dunr.
Harold R. Dunr.
Edwyn Harmer.
John Howell.
Robert Purdy.
Robert Pegg.
Gerald Whall.

In 1923, war memorials would have been seen as stone or marble edifices, along the lines of the one we have in Sheringham. No one, not even the most forward seeing prophet, could have foreseen that, one day, a war memorial could be digital (unless digital had the meaning of finger-like, which some memorials may appear to be). Clearly, what the legislators had in mind was that the memory of the sacrifices made in World War One would be perpetuated for posterity.

It could be argued that this publication is an appropriate adaption of a memorial, in keeping with modern technology, which very effectively honours those who gave their lives, as well as the many in the community who also served or were affected by the conflict. Young (and not so young) people today, do not connect readily with static, stone memorials, which in any case would simply give a list of names, which have little or any relevance to them. *Sheringham at War - 100 Years o*n can give far more details about the stories behind those names and will greatly expand the importance of the total price paid by a community (like so many others) such as Sheringham.

As a publication, it is vastly augmented by the website: **www.sheringhamww1project.uk**. Promoted through social media and the Council's own website, it is far more likely to attract those who need to be informed of the debt we owe to our forebears. Not ensuring that we make the community aware of the impact World War One had on Sheringham is not only a risk not worth taking, it risks dishonouring the memory of those the lawmakers of 1923 wanted us to remember and commemorate.

Gary Hughes, Simon Bottomley and Peter Farley

Sheringham War Memorial today

THEY SHALL GROW NOT OLD, AS WE THAT ARE LEFT GROW OLD:
AGE SHALL NOT WEARY THEM, NOR THE YEARS CONDEMN.
AT THE GOING DOWN OF THE SUN AND IN THE MORNING,
WE WILL REMEMBER THEM.

Over 40 million poppies are distributed by the Royal British Legion every year – a symbol of remembrance and hope

ADVERTISERS

We are grateful to our advertisers for financially supporting this publication

SHERINGHAM MUSEUM
at the MO

Step inside stunning galleries where you can walk amongst an extraordinary historic fleet of lifeboats and fishing boats. Here you will find the story of the town and its proud, brave and independent people. Packed with fascinating stories and interesting details.

EXPLORE

conserving & preserving

Funding raised by The National Lottery
and awarded by the Heritage Lottery Fund

heritage lottery fund
LOTTERY FUNDED

SHARE Museums East
a network of know how

LEST WE FORGET

LEST WE FORGET SHERINGHAM in WW1

SPECIAL EXHIBITION FREE ENTRY
10th - 11th November
Sheringham Museum

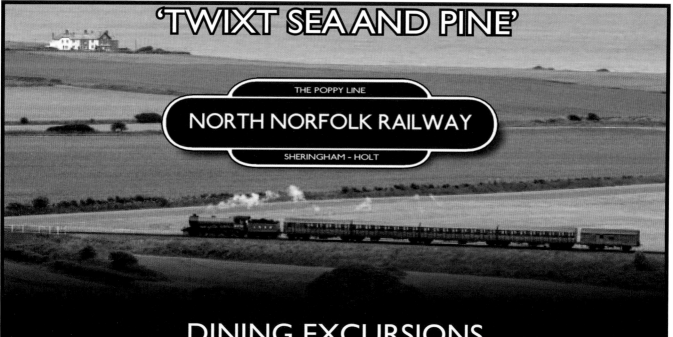

Silver and Ward are delighted to be supporting the Sheringham WW1 Project

Silver & Ward will continue to be one of the few solicitors to offer ALL the following services:

- **A FREE FIRST APPOINTMENT ON ALL LEGAL ISSUES**
- Exceeding the needs and expectations of our clients
- The same legal expertise as a city or larger local firm
- Providing the best service and solution to your legal problem
  at VERY COMPETITIVE RATES
- Home visits and disabled access and parking at our office
- Quality legal advice you can rely on
- Direct contact by phone, email or mobile for a prompt and efficient service.

We know what our clients need and expect
and we aim to exceed that, on all legal issues.
If you would like to make your

FIRST FREE APPOINTMENT
then please telephone **01263 823465**
or email clare@silverandward.co.uk.

Silver and Ward Ltd, 15A Cromer Road, Sheringham, NR26 8AB

"A FRESH APPROACH TO LAW"

clare@silverandward.co.uk   www.silverandward.co.uk

mackenziehotels.com

Frazers Restaurant

AA Rosette Award For Fine Dining ★★★

SEA MARGE
OVERSTRAND
01263 579579

Upchers Restaurant

AA Rosette Award For Fine Dining ★★★★

THE DALES COUNTRY HOUSE
UPPER SHERINGHAM
01263 824555

In 2 Blu Restaurant

★★★

THE LINKS COUNTRY PARK
WEST RUNTON
01263 838383

The Morley Club

The Morley Club was founded in December 1919 and has become one of the premium clubs in the county of Norfolk providing both a great sporting and social environment. Whether it's a drink in our fully licensed, air conditioned bar, a lunch time snack, a game of snooker, pool, bridge or bowls, The Morley Club has lots to offer for visitors and locals alike.

Club membership is £10 annually, the year starting 1st January. There is a temporary membership available for holiday makers, or if you wish to partake in an activity on a one off basis you can pay a £1 visitors fee, and the appropriate amount for the activity you wish to play.

You'll find us just off the main Sheringham to Cromer Road (A149). There is plenty of parking in the main town car park just round the corner. For information on any aspect regarding the club you can contact the various secretaries under each activity or the club manager, Liz Green on 01263 822087.

The club is open Monday to Saturday from 11am to 11pm. Sundays and Bank Holidays from 12am to 3pm.

LAWRENCES
Budgens

Discover Sheringham's locally owned and operated independent convenience store

- Great value everyday essentials
- Fresh fruit and vegetables
- Freshly-baked bread
- Meat and dairy

- Mouth-watering ready meals
- Beer and wine
- Local craft beers and produce including chutneys, jam and meats

Esso Service Station
16 Weybourne Road
Sheringham, NR26 8HF

COOK
Remarkable Food For Your Freezer

COSTA EXPRESS

THE NATIONAL LOTTERY

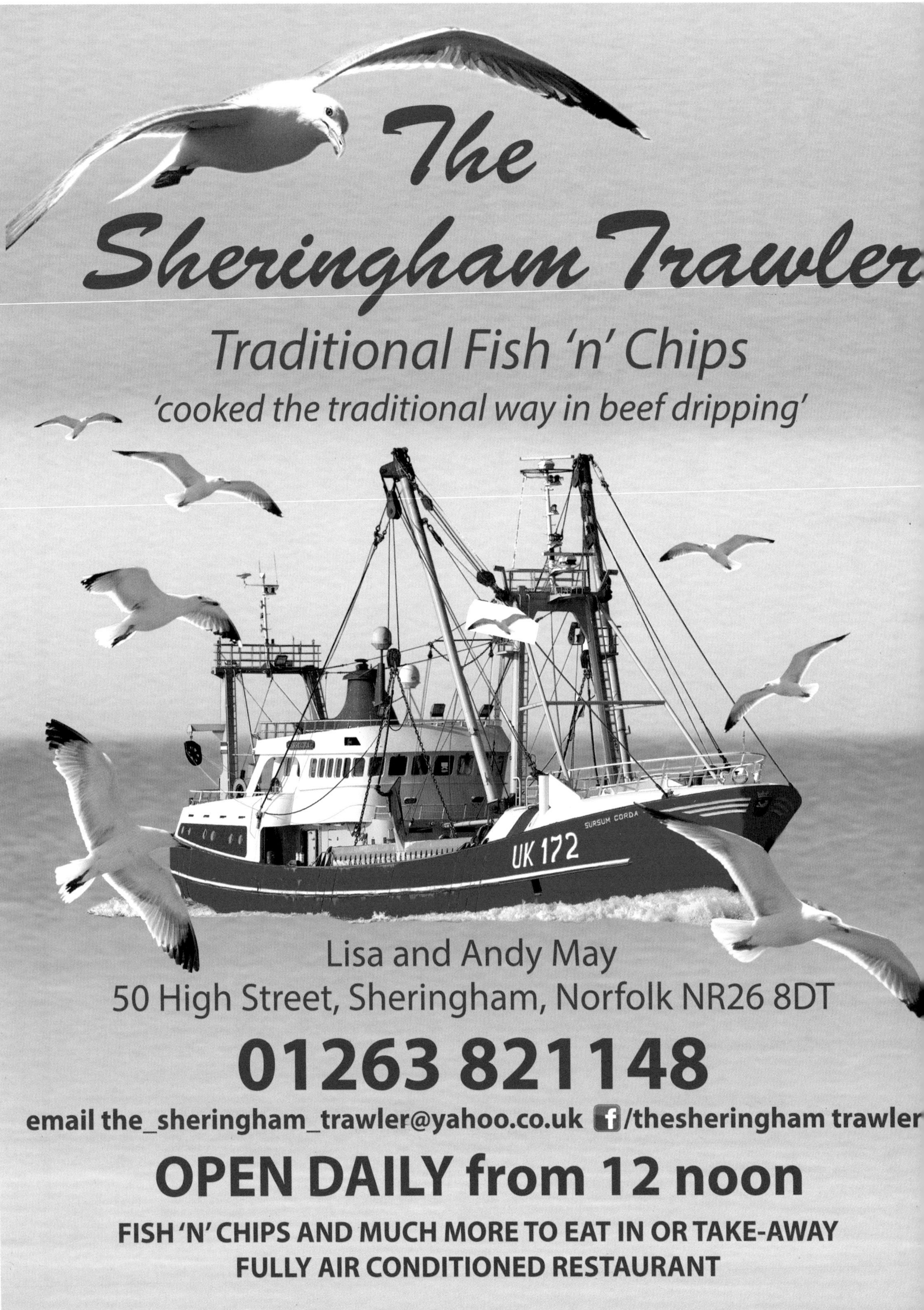
The Sheringham Trawler
Traditional Fish 'n' Chips
'cooked the traditional way in beef dripping'
SURSUM CORDA
UK 172
Lisa and Andy May
50 High Street, Sheringham, Norfolk NR26 8DT
01263 821148
email the_sheringham_trawler@yahoo.co.uk /thesheringham trawler
OPEN DAILY from 12 noon
FISH 'N' CHIPS AND MUCH MORE TO EAT IN OR TAKE-AWAY
FULLY AIR CONDITIONED RESTAURANT